IN A HUNDRED HUNDRED GRAVES

A BASQUE PORTRAIT

BOOKS IN THE BASQUE SERIES

Basque Nationalism
by Stanley G. Payne

Amerikanuak: Basques in the New World
by William A. Douglass and Jon Bilbao

Aurrera!: A Textbook for Studying Basque
by Linda White

Back to Bizkaia: A Basque-American Memoir
by Vince J. Juaristi

*The Basques, the Catalans, and Spain:
Alternative Routes to Basque Nationalization*
by Daniele Conversi

*Chorizos in an Iron Skillet: Memories and Recipes
from an American Basque Daughter*
by Mary Ancho Davis

The Circle of Mountains: A Basque Shepherding Community
by Sandra Ott

Deep Blue Memory
by Monique Laxalt Urza

An Enduring Legacy: The Story of Basques in Idaho
by John Bieter and Mark Bieter

Gernika, 1937: The Market Day Massacre
by Xabier Irujo

The Good Oak
by Martin Etchart

Reclaiming Basque: Language, Nation, and Cultural Activism
by Jacqueline Urla

The Basque Language
by Alan R. King

IN A HUNDRED HUNDRED GRAVES

A BASQUE PORTRAIT

ROBERT LAXALT

UNIVERSITY OF NEVADA PRESS

RENO & LAS VEGAS

THE BASQUE SERIES

University of Nevada Press, Reno, Nevada 89557 USA
www.unpress.nevada.edu
Copyright © 1972 by Robert Laxalt
All rights reserved
Manufactured in the United States of America

LIBRARY OF CONGRESS CATALOGING-IN-PUBLICATION DATA
Laxalt, Robert, 1923–2001
In a hundred graves; a Basque portrait. Reno,
University of Nevada Press, 1972.
146 p. 23 cm. (The Basque Series)
Autobiographical.
ISBN 978-0-87417-035-1 (cloth : alk. paper)
1. País Vasco Spain)—Social life and customs.
2. Laxalt, Robert, 1923–2001
I. Title.
DP302.B467L38   914.6'6   72-87404   MARC

University of Nevada Press Paperback Edition, 2016
ISBN: 978-1-943859-09-2 (pbk.: alk. paper)

This book has been reproduced as a digital reprint.

BOOKS BY ROBERT LAXALT

The Basque Hotel

Child of the Holy Ghost

A Man in the Wheatfield

The Governor's Mansion: A Novel

A lean Year and Other Stories

Dust Devils: A Novella

A Private War: An American Code Officer in the Belgian Congo

The Land of My Fathers: A Son Returns to the Basque Country

A Cup of Tea in Pamplona

Time of the Rabies: A Novella

Travels with my Royal: A Memoir of the Writing Life

Nevada: A History

Sweet Promised Land: 50th Anniversary Edition

Solitude: Are and Symbolism in the National Basque Monument

In a Hundred Graves: A Basque Portrait

FOR BRUCE AND NICK AND KRIS

Death in a
Basque Village

Someone is dying in the village tonight.

A little while after dusk, the bell in the village church began to toll and it has been tolling through the early hours of night. Like the beat of a faltering heart, its message sounds over the darkened rooftops of the village and into the taverns and the homes.

The few men in the taverns talk but little and there is no singing at all. In the homes, the Basque villagers eat their supper in silence, because what can one talk about when a deathbell is tolling.

Sometime in the night, I awoke thinking that my heart was pounding. But it was not my heart at all. It was the churchbell ringing out in a clamor. The angel of death had arrived.

Now, there is silence, absolute silence. And because I have come from a crowded place where death has lost its meaning, I lie awake in the dark and am filled with amazement.

Our Grand House—
Three Views

By village standards, our house is a grand house. It is big and has three stories and any number of little balconies. A sweep of lawn and a winding entrance separate it from the lane where the Basque *paysans* pass on the way to their farms.

I suppose it is rather impressive, but we have never considered it that at all. Our time in this land is only temporary, and after all, the house does not even belong to us.

My relatives are proud that we live in such a house. We are the American cousins, and they would have felt ashamed if we had lived in a poor house. For a while, they were a little jealous, too, because the house was finer and had more conveniences than their farmhouses. But they have come to be comfortable here when they visit.

Yesterday, a *paysan* from a remote mountain property came to the house on a matter of business, and I invited him in for a glass of wine. He was a spare man with a sun-darkened face and big calloused hands. Because he had on rough clothes, he was reluctant to come inside.

We sat in the dining room, and he perched on the edge of his chair and in the manner of farm men, planted one elbow staunchly on the table. While we talked, his eyes roved wonderingly over every part of the dining room—the patterned paper on the walls, the gleaming mirror over the buffet, the chandelier over the table.

The affair of the house had become embarrassing, and I felt that I should apologize in some way to this man. But before I could speak, the *paysan* shook his head and said to me, "Do you know? I couldn't go to sleep in a house like this."

School in a Fortress

Our children go to school in the old stone fortress that dominates the village. In order to go from our house to the fortress, they must walk down a long lane overgrown with brier and berry bushes, and then climb the steep road upwards to the top of the hill. On these autumn mornings, the hill where the fortress stands is nearly always shrouded with mist.

They pass beside ghosted ramparts where greenery grows through the chinks in the walls. They walk under mossy oaks and along deep moats covered with velvet grass. And finally, they cross over a drawbridge of wood and rusted chains that creaks beneath their footsteps.

I have said to them that it must be a great adventure to go to school in a fortress. And they have said to me that school in a fortress means cold and gloomy rooms.

I suppose they are right. But when the memory of cold rooms has been forgotten, I think the memory of ghosted ramparts and a creaking drawbridge will remain.

The House of No Name

As each man has a house that he loves, so have I mine.

I found it this morning when walking along a road I had never taken before. The house is really not so far from the village, but it seems to be very far away from anywhere. It lies in a patch of ground between the forest and a stream that slaps and gurgles its way along to join the mother Nive. It is so perfectly encircled by forest and stream and a brow of green mountain that it is like an island on the sea.

The house is made of stone, and it is very old. I can tell that from the waving line of the roof, and also from the tiles that have been replaced one by one so many times that they lie on the house like a patchwork quilt in red and black.

The house faces to the east, so that in the morning sun the whitewashed stone of its front is dazzling. Over the long years, a grapevine has made its way across the front of the house, winding under the window and over the doorway. Its leaves cover the keystone above the doorway, obscuring the old name of the house and the year in which it was built. I am glad for that, because now I can pretend it is a house of no name.

There are two little gardens beside the house. One is for beauty and one is for nurture. There are roses and tulips and hortensia in the flower garden. There are tomatoes and carrots and potatoes and lettuce and I am not sure what else in the other. But I am sure of one thing: a weed would not dare intrude into those neat and ordered rows.

Beyond the garden, there is an orchard of apple and cherry and plum trees. On the grass beneath them, chickens and pink pigs cluck and root in their morning feeding, unmindful of each other. And beyond the orchard, there is a tiny vineyard. It is thick with leaf and the vines are gnarled and old, and I am sure they will provide good wine.

From the bridge, I cannot see much of the stone barn behind the house. There is a sod path leading up to the doorway, and the doorway is dark so that one cannot see inside. But I know anyway that the mangers must be clean and warm.

When I lingered on the bridge, I did not know there was anyone about. But then I looked down, and there was an old man sitting on the warm brown earth beside the stream. A bundle of willows was at his feet, and he was weaving a basket. He worked as unhurriedly as if time did not exist.

And as I watched him weave, I fell under the spell, too, and was drawn the rest of the way into the life of the house between the stream and the mountain, and for that moment forgot time and destinations and the worried world I had left behind.

A Lesson
of the Eyes

Dominika is my daughters' playmate. She is not very pretty, really, because she has a big nose and eyes that protrude.

But she has golden hair that hangs in ringlets over her shoulders. Her hair is so beautiful that one cannot speak of Dominika without speaking of her hair. Always, the two must go together, and so the illusion of beauty persists.

She lives with her grandmother and grandfather in a little farmhouse down the lane. They work hard and they are proper people. The grandfather's only excess is to allow himself one aperitif too many after Sunday Mass in the village. When he passes our house on his way home for the big Sunday lunch, his beret is a little askew on his gray head, and his stringbean figure weaves slightly. But he has worked hard all week and can take his Sunday cup in good conscience.

Dominika's grandparents care for her well. I can never remember a time when her hair has not been curled and her worn smock has not been clean. No one can take them to task for that. I know now why this is necessary.

We understood each other in the beginning, Dominika and I. When she came to our house to play, she was polite and distant. We had not exchanged a dozen words. But that is Basque.

The fact that Dominika lived with her grandparents had not struck me as strange. I had assumed her mother and father were dead. And then I overheard one day that her mother was not dead, but lived somewhere in the village. I wondered about this, but one learns in a village that it is bad grace to inquire into such matters. And one learns also that in time, the unasked question will be answered.

When finally I discovered her story, it was really not that important. She was illegitimate. No more than that, and my heart went out to her.

It is the American thing to do, to show by an overt action that we understand. So when next the children came into the house to play, I offered Dominika one piece of candy more than the others.

It was a lesson of the eyes, with no words pronounced. Dominika refused the candy, and there were suddenly a thousand miles between us.

Dominika has had little to do with me since, this child of ten, who is older and wiser than I.

The Tilemaker

Down the long lane, I had seen nothing of the morning. I did not see the tilemaker, either, except vaguely to notice a man replacing the dark tiles on the roof of a house, and that he was whistling.

As I went on, it occurred to me how very long it had been since I had heard a man whistling. At a bend in the lane, where I could stand and he could not see me, I stopped to listen. The tilemaker's whistling was like the notes of a flute gone wild, soaring to such marvelous heights that I fancied the birds had fallen quiet to listen, too.

Piece by piece, the tilemaker repaired the dark places in the roof, and in me.

Perpetual Spring

The women do their wash at a perpetual spring.

The spring is protected by a roof that rests on four oaken beams, and both the roof and the beams are blackened with age. The water from the spring pours into a long wooden trough and out again, so that it is always fresh. Slanting slabs of stone rest on the trough like washboards all in a line. The women scrub and slap their wash on the stone slabs, and then rinse it clean in the running water beneath.

The women who gather at the perpetual spring are of many types. And yet, because they have the same gestures and expressions born out of life in a village, they seem to resemble each other. There are square and solid farm women with round faces and ruddy cheeks, and forearms grooved like a man's. There are willowy girls with auburn hair and hazel eyes or black hair and blue eyes, with rich color in their cheeks and music in their voices. And there are old crones in long black dresses, a yellow tooth or two dangling, and voices dry as rasps.

The women gather at the spring in rain or sunshine, and always the start of every conversation must be the weather. If the day is bad, then no one can remember when it has ever been good. And if the day is fair, then the weather has been beautiful forever.

When they talk, the women deal always in discretion, because to do otherwise is not considered proper. A morsel offered here, and a morsel there. The love affairs of the young, a marriage of convenience, a worthy child and an ungrateful one, a birth to be and an approaching death, the eternal lament of money.

All things are in time revealed. The fabric of life in the village is spun out at the perpetual spring.

Our Town Crier

The town crier is an important personage in the village. It is always an event when he makes his rounds, and what he has to proclaim is important. Make no mistake about that.

The town crier is a fat man with a florid face and long flowing moustache that makes one think he might have served in Napoleon's army. (And there are some who say he is just about that old.) He wears a blue uniform with red lapels and gold tassels. The uniform is looking a little faded and worn these days, but it is still very impressive.

When he emerges from the hôtel de ville, which is the seat of village government, he strides importantly to the middle of the square. In his left hand he holds his proclamation rolled in a scroll. And in his right, he grasps a brass trumpet. He plants his feet firmly apart and makes a blast on his trumpet that Gabriel would envy. (And there are some who say that if he does not arouse Gabriel's envy, he certainly arouses him.)

When the last note is dying away, the town crier unfurls the scroll and reads its contents aloud. He has a magnificent voice that is a delight to hear. The villagers who happen to be passing through the square always stop whatever they are doing, and the shopkeepers on the other side of the square always come out in their aprons to listen.

When he is done, the town crier carefully rolls up the scroll and goes off down the street to proclaim again. If he is making his rounds on a holiday, there are children who follow him, so that soon he resembles the Pied Piper of Hamelin.

When he has finished with the main street, the town crier passes through the great arched doorway of the rampart and into the old fortified quarter. At the sound of his trumpet, shutters fly open on both sides of the cobblestone street, and housewives in black lean out to listen.

Sometimes he announces a decree, sometimes a marriage or a death, and sometimes only that a fish merchant from the sea will be here on Friday. And sometimes when he reads a date, he makes a mistake. The villagers forgive him for this, because he is not telling them anything that they do not know already. They also forgive him because the town crier does not know how to read.

Law

The bracken grows on the hillsides, and in the summer its green leaves resemble a child's drawing of a Christmas tree.

But the bracken grows too swiftly, and by the end

of summer it threatens to crowd out the grass. So, in the autumn, the farmers burn the bracken when it has rusted.

In the village, the French gendarmes walk by in the night, shaking their heads. The Basque people wait until they have passed, and then they laugh merrily.

In the black autumn night, the entire valley is ringed with separate fires. Each fire is like a mouth with its edges upturned, so that it seems as though all the hillsides are laughing.

No wonder they are.

I was with my cousin at dusk when we fired his hillside, and he said, "You know, of course, that this is against the law."

"Then why do you do it?"

"So that my animals will have grass to eat in the spring."

"But it's still against the law."

"Yes, but it's not a good law."

Stone Huts

The first time I made the perilous ascent from the valley floor and came upon the stone huts in their high place, I thought for a moment that I was disjointed in time. They are not the kind of habitation one's eyes are used to. There is something about them that is much too old.

On the green hump of mountain above the timberline, each of them is crouched in its own lee, protected from the storms. They lie just beneath the brutal rim of the Pyrenees.

Below the hump of mountain and the stone huts, there are steeply descending slopes gashed with chasms and cascades of flashing water. The slopes are covered with forests of oak and chestnut whose trunks are crusted with lichen. Under the trees there are deep growths of bracken and gorse. These are not joyful forests. The birds nest on the outer fringes near the sunlight, and only beasts and creatures of superstition are said to know the secrets of the interior darkness. As in times before, the forests serve as a barrier from the world below.

It is claimed that the stone huts were once inhabited by the ancestors of the Basques, spear-bearing men who wore skins of wolves and bear, a race of hunters who dismayed Roman invaders by their code of suicide before capture, whose sons crept through enemy lines at night to kill their fathers and so spare them the shame of being prisoner.

In the vicinity of the stone huts, there are two objects that give credence to this claim. One is a great cave perched on a high point of land. The path to it is narrow as a knife and as treacherous. There are no other approaches. The cave is honeycombed with tunnels whose openings fall away to precipices. The cave is a natural fortress.

Another object lies concealed in the forest. It is an altar to a pagan deity, a crude table rock of worship set on two stone uprights. The name of the deity has been forgotten in the memory of the Basques, but as long as the altar stands, the presence of the deity remains in some mute and disturbing way. The only beings who visit it now are the *pottok,* shaggy little vestiges of prehistoric horse such as I have seen etched on the walls of ancient caves. They nibble at the grass in the clearing, and by their presence, keep the bracken from encroaching too near the altar.

Eyes of the Dove

The path on which we mounted was flanked by rusted fern, and overhead there was a crimson and gold canopy of beech and chestnut trees. Dew dripped down from dying leaves, and the air was filled with the sweet smell of death.

When my cousin and I crossed the hump of the mountain and came into the pass, the old stone cabin with its swayback roof lay below us, almost hidden in the embrace of gnarled oaks.

Even though they had been pointed out to me, I could not at first see the nets. Then there was a breath of wind, and by the shimmering movement, I saw them. They were like immense cobwebs, so finely woven that their strands had caught the dew. Strung on slender poles, they reared to a terrifying height. Stretched side by side from low ground up the slopes, they blocked the narrow pass with an invisible barrier.

There was a giant oak on the descending slope beyond the nets, and in its topmost branches there was a tree hut. This was the Tower of Death where a hunter waited with the whittled wooden projectiles that when thrown resemble a falcon in flight. A man's grinning face hung disembodiedly in the black opening of the tree hut.

"What luck?" my cousin called up.

"With this weather?" the hunter in the hut said. "I could just as well be next to the fire."

"If you're cold," my cousin said, "I will take your place for a while."

"Listen," said the hunter. "As soon as I left here, a thousand doves would surely come. And I and my progeny would live a thousand years before we heard the end of it."

On the side of the cabin that looked downward into the ravine, there was a wooden barricade. The barricade was camouflaged with fern, and eyeslits for the hunters had been carved into the wood. Here also was the great wooden lever that tripped the nets.

Inside the cabin, the fireplace was drafting badly and the room was thick with woodsmoke. There were designs etched in charcoal on the bare walls, and each design was of a dove and beneath it, in round thousands, the number of doves that had been taken that particular season.

The men sitting on the axe-hewn benches around the fireplace were talking in Basque. Their berets were tipped back and they sat with elbows planted on knees or with hands resting in their laps, staring into the flames. They were villagers with a house-share in the hunt, handed down to them through the centuries. The only one who did not have a house-share was Joanes, who was big and foolish and every-one's handyman. He was there because of a particular talent.

I recognized some of them. There was one who had the name of a gossip, and another with a sharp and aristocratic face, who was a smuggler.

But the one who spoke to me first was an old man with a seamed face who had spent ten years in Amer-ica herding sheep. "I would be there now if I didn't have a property that I had to come back to," he said. "I was a pure American. I even learned how to speak English."

"What good has speaking English done you here?" said the gossip, who had a fleshy face and tiny blue eyes.

"It has nothing to do with good," said the old shepherd. "Just the fact of knowledge." He grinned slyly. "I came back with knowledge and a fine pair of American pants."

"And money," said the gossip.

"Well of course, money," said the shepherd.

"And bad health."

"If I had bad health, I wouldn't be up here."

A man with a ruddy blade face spoke up for the shepherd. "Your health is not so good that you can accuse others of having bad health," he said to the gossip.

"And why shouldn't my health be bad after five years in a German prison camp?" the gossip said. He deliberated for a moment, and then he made his decision. "At least no one can say I stayed home to traffic with the Germans in the occupation." With one finger, he pulled down the skin under his eye until the red showed. "Don't worry. You were seen."

The man with the blade face glanced at me in agonized humiliation. "You didn't have it so hard in prison," he said to the gossip. "You came back with a big belly."

The old shepherd wagged his head sorrowfully. "There are many things a man will do when his children are hungry," he said. But the man with the blade face had already withdrawn into sullen silence, and I knew at that moment he would never in his life forgive the gossip's destruction of his name.

Joanes, too, was uncomfortable. "The fire is drawing better," he said, inclining his head toward me. "We're going to have hunting yet. Perhaps you'll see something after all."

At his words, the smuggler got up from the bench and went out the door to look at the feather impaled on a stick. Clapping his hands together, he said, "For once in your life, Joanes, you are right. The wind is changing."

The old shepherd had just put a cigarette in his mouth. He offered me the pack. "Do you want a De Gaulle?"

I took one warily. "Why do you call them De Gaulles?"

"Because he is on pension now and De Gaulle buys his cigarettes for him," said the gossip. "And that's why he has to vote for De Gaulle, too."

The old shepherd shrugged. "Yes, but he also sent the bad weather up here. So I don't think I'll vote for him."

The smuggler had been listening to the exchange. "That's a good one," he said. "I haven't heard that one before." His quick eyes narrowed as though he had thought of something. "Joanes!" he said sharply.

Joanes raised his shaggy head like a sheepdog who has just come awake. "I'm here," he said.

The smuggler had crossed to the wooden table where there were bottles of Pernod and glasses, and a Basque wineskin made of goathide. "Well, will you come *here* a minute?" he said, taking up the wineskin.

Joanes stood up uncertainly, fingering the buttonless top of his shirt, and finally shuffled in his wooden shoes to the table.

"Our friend from America would like to know how one drinks from a *chahakoa*," he said. "I'm not adept enough to teach him. As a master in the art of all drinking, would you show him how it is done?"

Joanes colored with the compliment. "It's a simple thing," he said, "but of course I will do it."

"You are truly a gentleman," said the smuggler gravely. Before handing the wineskin to Joanes, he turned to me. "Note how he does this. The right hand at the throat of the wineskin and the left hand squeezing the bottom."

Joanes did not see it, but the others in the room did. In the instant that the smuggler had turned away from Joanes, he gave the nozzle below the jet a turn to loosen it.

Joanes took a wide stance and upended the wineskin, and a thin red stream played expertly from the jet into his mouth. At the same time, big drops dribbled from the loosened nozzle onto his shirtfront. Lowering the wineskin, Joanes smiled proudly. The smile faded and a look of consternation came into Joanes's face. He raised his hand slowly to touch his dampened shirt. Then, recovering himself, he said politely, "It's good wine."

"But what is this?" said the smuggler, poking at Joanes's shirtfront. "I thought you were proficient with the wineskin."

Joanes leaned forward to whisper something into the smuggler's ear.

"Oh, but you are wrong," said the smuggler. "Don't pretend to save my feelings. My wineskin is not faulty, and I will prove it to you."

He took the wineskin from Joanes, tightened the nozzle with a hidden movement, and drank from it without spilling a drop. "It works fine," he said, loosening the nozzle again. "Try it and see for yourself."

At the end of the third exchange, Joanes's shirt-front was a great red smear and the smuggler was not bothering to conceal his laughter anymore. Joanes went to sit at his place beside the fire. "I cannot understand it," he said in a destroyed voice. "I have drunk from the *chahakoa* since I was a child. I thought I knew how, but obviously I was mistaken."

The shepherd looked at me embarrassedly. "What can you expect from a smuggler?" he said in English. "It's a shame you had to see it."

The shepherd was pensive for a moment, staring into the flames. "Listen," he said. "The hunting will begin very soon now. Before it does, there is something else you must understand. Today, you have seen cruelty. You must be very careful not to confuse it with what you are about to see, because the hunt is much older than cruelty."

The sound of the distant horn hung in the air even after the hunters had plunged out of the cabin. My friend and I followed, ducking into the opening of the covered barricade. Joanes was standing beside the great wooden lever that would trip the nets, and his hands were already gripping the handle.

I pressed my face against the eyeslit in the barricade. I saw the flight, dark specks in a broken arc coming into the funnel of the pass. Its coming was leisurely and unsuspecting. Then, as though part of the flight had recalled a warning out of the ages, the arc began to come apart and one segment of it veered away to the side. In the barricade, someone swore.

Then, magically, a long pole with a fluttering white cloth thrust out of the bracken on a high slope. The segment veered back and the flight was corrected.

But the doves were frightened now. They were coming swiftly and the arc was no longer an arc, but two hundred doves banded together in a formless mass. They were almost abreast of the Tower of Death, so close that I could hear the heartbeat drumming of their wings.

The white projectiles hurtled out of the tower like falcons whirling down in attack. At sight of them, the flight became a single thing that reared up with hands outstretched in horror. Then, as if the rearing had exposed the soft vulnerability of their undersides, the doves dived down close to the ground and came the rest of the way to the waiting nets in a blur of swiftness.

In one instant, the flight had been a thing of one mind and one movement. In the next, it was a soundless explosion of feathers and no movement at all. The birds hung in awkward disarray in the webbed strands of the net, as though they had been pasted against a canvas of sky. Joanes jerked the levers and the nets came tumbling down, to settle like invisible blankets over the doves.

After the others had gone, I trailed out of the barricade and went to stand at the edge of the nets. The villagers were walking carefully over the webbing, disengaging the birds from the strands that enmeshed them, handing them to Joanes to kill, tossing them afterwards into a growing pile.

There was a movement at my feet, and it was a dove. Reaching down, I worked him gently through the webbing. The eyes of the dove were open and stunned, yet seeing. He lay without moving in my hands, and through the tips of my fingers, it seemed that I felt not only the flow of life but the throbbing tempers of the distant northlands from which he had come.

"Here, my friend," said Joanes. "I will kill him for you." He took the dove and lifted it to his mouth. The iron jaws closed on its neck and there was a tiny crunch of bone, and the dove lay again in my hands. The life and the tempers were ebbing away. When the dove was an empty clump of feathers, I walked to the pile and threw him onto it.

Kashinto

Kashinto is a Bohemian.

He is a boy, but nobody seems to know exactly how old he is, because nobody cares. He is dark-skinned and dirty and has black oval eyes, and his ragged clothes hang shapelessly on his body. Still, he has a sunny smile, and I had taken to waving when I passed by with the car.

The children say that Kashinto is very stupid, but perhaps they say that because he cannot talk. There is something wrong with his tongue, and he makes a gobbling noise when he tries to speak. The children say that the boys in school have to beat him nearly every day because he hits the girls. But it may be that he hits the girls after the boys have beaten him.

Kashinto lives with his father and mother and brothers and sisters in a little house that sits on the spine of a hill opposite from us, so that we can see it in all seasons. In winter, when the cold gray rains are sheeting down, the house has a forlorn aspect. The tiles on its roof are old and cracked, and the whitewash on its walls takes on the grayness of the rain.

In the evenings I can see the family gathering to the house from several directions. The children come home from school first, and they make tiny figures struggling against the sky on the crest of the hill. Then comes Kashinto's mother from her daily round of begging at doors and scavenging in trashcans, and her figure against the sky is bent with its load. And last comes Kashinto's father on the footpath from the forest beyond the house, his two woodsman's axes crossed on his shoulder.

After he has come, a curl of blue smoke rises from the chimney and there is a glow of light from the one window that looks down at us. I think the light comes only from the chimney glow, because when the smoke dies, the light in the window dies, too.

The Basques in the village say that the family does not have to live that way anymore, because the government sees to that. They say the father and the mother spend their dole on liquor, and that they get drunk every Saturday night and have glorious fights, out of which they seem to harbor no memory of ill will. The Basques in the village remark on this with amusement, because they cannot understand it.

Once, when I was walking in the forest, I came upon Kashinto's father at his woodchopping. Because of the ringing of the axe, he did not hear my approach, and at first he was startled. And then he doffed his beret and stood in embarrassment when I spoke to him. We talked for a moment about the hardness of the wood, and then there was no more to say, and so I went on, wishing that I had not stopped.

I wish that I had not met Kashinto, either. But some things are inevitable. After all, one does not pass a boy walking home in the rain with a great armload of bread that is beginning to fall apart with water.

Even then it took some convincing, because he stared at the open door and the gleaming interior as though he were paralyzed. When the car began to move and the bushes and the trees whirred past him, he lost control of himself. He dropped the bread and beat on the soft seat and made gobbling noises of pleasure in his throat. I let him off at the junction of the lane and the path that mounted to his little house.

After that, it seemed that I could never pass the junction without finding him there waving me down. But I never stopped for Kashinto again. At first, he was puzzled and then he watched me pass with brooding and sullen eyes. But enough time has gone by now, and as in the beginning, he simply waves and smiles a sunny smile. I think that he has forgotten the shunning and remembers only the experience.

And as for me, I cannot understand why I have never stopped for Kashinto again. Perhaps because in the eyes of the village, I had done a forbidden thing. Perhaps because Kashinto tried to possess me. But I think really that it was because Kashinto could not know pride.

A Basque Kitchen

In my aunt's farmhouse there is a parlor with frigid stone floors and family pictures and a proper table where company is received. And so were we received in the beginning. But we have been here long enough now to be admitted to the heart of the house, which is the kitchen.

In the kitchen, there are benches and a long wooden table for meals. The table is scarred, but the wood is oak and so the scars are soft. From the beams above hang magnificent hams with the white ball of a joint showing, ropes of sausages, strings of reddening peppers, and wreaths of garlic. They fill the kitchen with their aroma.

The kitchen has its own heart, and that is the fireplace. It is a massive fireplace open on three sides, so that the fire seems almost to be burning within the room. Its mantle is covered with a hanging fringe of white linen embroidered with threads of red and blue. Pewter candlesticks and red copper trays rest on the mantle.

The back of the fireplace is of patterned white tiles. A heavy chain from which pots were once suspended disappears upward into a cavernous chimney blackened by the smoke of centuries.

We gather often around the fireplace at night. Sometimes we talk of family and the life my mother found in America. And sometimes we talk of my father and his life as a sheepherder in the hills. And always, there are questions about Basques who left the village as boys and never came home again. What we are really doing is bridging impossible oceans, but there is pleasure in it.

We have talked around the fireplace on spring nights when the wind sighs with a human voice, and on autumn nights when the wind moans sadly, as though preparing the earth for death to come. And then there are the winter nights when the wind outside screeches and assails the stone walls of the house and makes the upstairs flooring creak with forgotten ghosts. The kitchen is thick with gloom, and we cup our chins in our hands and stare into the flames, and are content to say nothing.

Acceptance

The regard with which they greeted me in the gray wintry morning could not be called hostility. Rather, it was that measure of distance, of lives and experiences unshared, that Basques will throw up when there is an intruder present. This was a family affair, and I have come to know these things of family well.

Still, my neighbor—the only one of the men that I knew—had invited me to the slaughter in good heart. And so I bore the scrutiny of the other men and played the game of distance.

It was a family of big men. No one could have mistaken the fact that the same blood ran through all of them. It was an unlikely combination of fine dark faces growing out of burly shoulders and thick chests. They were all dressed alike, with berets and heavy sweaters, and baggy blue cotton pants stuffed into black rubber boots. They spoke little to me and scarcely at all to each other.

They had come from other farms to help with the slaughter, and there was much work to be done before they could go home. The man who was to be the butcher sharpened his knives, the others hauled out the slaughter block, and then together we went to get the pig.

When I was a boy and saw things led to die, what baffled me always was that they had not the least anticipation of their fate. They could not comprehend what was going to happen until it was happening. Not so with a pig. Brutish and unlovely, he has nevertheless the capacity for anticipation.

Though he had been taken from his pen a hundred times before, he knew on this morning that we had come to fetch him to slaughter. From the moment we gathered around his pen in the gloom of the barn, he began to circle his wooden prison at a run, snuffling and grunting in panic. Once, he tried to crash his way through the heavy timbers that hemmed him in.

At first sight of him, it did not seem possible that even these big men could hold him down. But this was an old business with them, and they knew what they were about. A loop of rope was laid on the floor of the pen, and inevitably in the pig's circling, a hind foot stepped into the snare. In an instant, the pig was floundering on three legs. In another instant, a man had leaped into the pen and forced a harsh cord into the pig's mouth and around his lower jaw. Other hands grasped onto ears and tail, and the pig was captive. Only then did he begin to squeal.

Down the long dark corridor of the barn, the pig fought against his fate, twisting and squirming, heaving us against the wooden stalls. But what was to come was in the future, and the painful cord around his jaw was now, and so finally he went. His greatest protest was in his squealing. It was unbelievable that one animal could make so much noise.

The slaughter block, solidly supported by oak legs and black with old stains, lay just beyond the door of the barn. Beside it stood the man who was to be the butcher. With his black beret and a dark apron that covered him from neck to ankles, he resembled a patient executioner. An old woman in long black, with a child's smile on her face, had come out of the house. She was holding a deep pan in one hand and a wooden ladle in the other.

When the pig emerged from the darkness into the cold daylight and saw the slaughter block and the waiting man and the waiting woman, he went insane. He would not be led further by the cord around his jaw, and for a moment, it seemed that he would shake himself free from all of us. Without a word between them, because this was an old business, too, the men reached under the pig and caught hold of his feet on the opposite side, and heaved. The pig fell mightily. Before he could get up again, his front legs and his hind legs had been trussed together. We carried him the rest of the way to the slaughter block.

It was quickly done. Hardly had the pig settled on the block than the knife stabbed down. The blade disappeared in his throat and made a quick circle, and a plug of skin and flesh popped out onto the ground. There was a mortal scream from the pig, and then black blood—turning to red as it touched the air—pumped out in a jet.

The woman had been waiting with her pan. She caught the stream, and bending over, began to stir with her wooden ladle. She smiled and nodded in satisfaction at the fact that the blood was not clotting.

The red stream flowed on and on. Yet, when it seemed the pig must surely be dead, and we had relaxed our holds on him, he unleashed an agonized scream of protest that was louder than all the rest. Before we could contain him, he had almost thrown himself off the block and had showered us with blood in the process. But that was his last scream.

Afterwards, when the pig had been lowered to the ground and covered with straw and set afire so as to burn off his hair, all the men gathered in a circle around the flames. The old woman brought glasses and a bottle. Bruised and spattered with blood, we drank wine over the smouldering heap that had been our adversary, and grinned at each other like old friends.

The Basque Troubador

My cousin and I had come down to the village after a day in the high, wild passes of the Pyrenees. It was nightfall, and there was a drizzling rain. We were wet and cold, and we stopped at a little tavern for a warming drink.

There had been a market that day, and the tavern was crowded with those *paysans* who had stayed late and were now faced with the prospect of outwaiting the rain. And as on market days, they were in noisy good humor. We found a place at the end of the bar, next to a mountain of a man with a ruddy face and a beret tipped back on his head. He and his comrade were trading stories, and every once in a while a rich laugh would come burbling up from jowly depths.

My cousin and I sipped a steaming mixture of coffee and brandy. *"Bertzolari,"* my cousin said in a low voice.

The word rang a bell somewhere in my uncertain Basque vocabulary. "Troubadour," my cousin explained, inclining his head toward the man's broad back. "He is a troubadour."

"Will he sing?" I asked.

My cousin shrugged. "Perhaps. But I don't think so."

The door to the tavern opened, and a figure came in out of the darkness, shaking the water from his umbrella. He wore the unmistakable garb of the shepherd, a wide beret, leggings wrapped tightly around his lower legs, and a long blue cape for a raincoat. His face was of the ancient Basque type, long and razor-lean, and there was a pride almost to arrogance in his bearing. He waved in answer to the greetings, and his black eyes flicked over the bar. When his gaze came to the huge *paysan* standing beside us, it stopped. He nodded with dignity, hooked the handle of his umbrella into the collar of his cape, and walked to the other end of the bar.

"Ah," my cousin said. "There will be singing, all right."

The noise in the tavern resumed, but now there was an undercurrent of expectation running through the laughter. Somewhere down the bar, someone sang a snatch of song, and another joined in. There were hoots of disapproval, because it was badly sung. I learned later that it was supposed to be.

"We are in song," my cousin whispered. "Soon, it will begin."

I looked at the *paysan* standing next to us. He was hunched over the bar, but in an easy attitude of waiting. His eyes were crinkled in flesh, and there was a mischievous smile on his lips. The transition from rough music to the business at hand was a subtle one. The little bursts of song and the cries of derision moved down the bar, like erratic descending notes on a keyboard.

The chill that coursed my back was not from the cold. Out of this burly giant came a tenor voice that was beautiful. Without looking up, and still hunched over the bar, he began to sing a story of a young shepherd fated to live forever in the cruel crags and swirling night mists of the high mountains. He dwelt at length upon the miseries of the youth, whose only moments of happiness came when, on clear nights, he could look down into the valley and see the warm light that peeped from the window of the house of a *paysan*, and contemplate all the familial joy and comfort that the light meant.

When he finished, there was a roar of bravos for the *paysan* and mockery for the life of a shepherd. My cousin rubbed his hands together. "That was delicious. He is in good form tonight."

The laughter had not even died down when the shepherd's response stilled the rest of it. He sang in a rich baritone, and, unlike the *paysan*, he stood dramatically facing the villagers, with one hand holding the bar and the other cocked on his hip, so that his cape flared out behind him.

For a moment it seemed that the shepherd was but adding to the *paysan*'s story. His song began with the young shepherd on his high rock, sorrowfully regarding the faraway light in the darkness. Then, with sudden resolve, the young shepherd decided to descend to the valley and peek through the window so that he could see the joys he was missing. Instead of the blissful scene he had expected, he saw an untidy kitchen, brawling children, and the final disappointment—the *paysan*'s wife beating him over the head with a broom for drinking too late with his comrades after market.

The shepherd was nearly finished with his response before it came to me that he had not only turned the *paysan*'s own story against him, but had done so without changing the melody or the rhyme.

When the shepherd finished his response and his champions had shouted out their approval, a silence fell over the tavern. It was complete and unexpected on the heels of so much sound and noise. As if in a play, the black-garbed villagers turned to their drinks, struck silent attitudes of thought, or spoke to each other in low tones, savoring verses from the exchange.

Next to us, the *paysan* hunched over the bar. But now his head was sunk deeper between his shoulders, and the expression of good humor was sharpened by deep furrows of concentration on his brow. He had need to think.

The shepherd had not changed his position at all, but still stood facing the room with his cape flared out behind him, staring ahead but seeing nothing in the intensity of his own thought. It was so quiet that one could hear the rustling of the open fire in the family room that adjoined the tavern.

"I think the shepherd has got your man on the run," I whispered to my cousin.

"He is not my man," said my cousin, offended. "I make it a practice to be impartial in these affairs. However, the shepherd takes himself too seriously for my taste. I think he fancies himself to be another Etchahoun."

"I remember that name," I said. "Once in America my father sang the verses of a contest between Etchahoun and another man."

"Ochalde," my cousin said. "It was such a meeting as this. They were the best of their time. Etchahoun was from the mountains, and Ochalde from the valley land. They met in a tavern when they were very old. What they sang was good, and it was remembered. But for my taste, the best of Etchahoun's verses came from the tragedy in his youth. Do you know the story?"

"No. I don't know that much about him."

"When Etchahoun was a young man," my cousin said, "his wife put horns on his head. So he lay in wait one night with a gun beside the bridge over which his wife's lover was to pass. In his passion, he altogether forgot that he had made a rendezvous to meet his best friend at the same bridge. A figure came in the darkness, and Etchahoun fired his gun. When he approached the dying man, it was to see that he had shot his friend.

"He fled to the high mountains to take refuge at the campfire of the shepherd boys, his hands still stained with the blood of his friend. This happened nearly one hundred and fifty years ago. And the story he sang in his heartbreak was remembered and brought down by the shepherd boys and is still sung today in the Basque country. It is very beautiful."

There was a shuffling of feet that broke the silence in the tavern. Nodding to the villagers as if heeding a signal, the shepherd began to sing. It was time for the tempo to be quickened to verse against verse. It was the shepherd's turn to start the exchange and thus to choose the rhyme and melody. In contrast to the slow, mocking cadence of the first round, he chose a rhythm that was quick and decisive. Since his was the opening thrust, he was bent on keeping the *paysan* on the defensive.

For a while, he succeeded. He sang of the young

shepherd returning to his mountains borne down with the disillusionment of what he had seen in the *paysan's* house. Because the *paysan* had to continue the thread of what the shepherd had sung, it seemed that he was forced to agree. In his first response, the *paysan* admitted that what the young shepherd had seen was true, and in the second, he commiserated with the unhappy youth. Sensing something, the shepherd pursued his theme warily. He told of the young shepherd's returning to his lofty peaks and noticing, as if for the first time, the peace and beauty of the starry night that was his realm.

Still, the *paysan* followed. He told of the henpecked *paysan's* decision to run away to the mountains and find there the peace of a shepherd's life. Now, the shepherd realized that there was a trap afoot, but because of the *paysan's* agreement with everything he was saying, and because there could be no hesitation in the exchange, he seemed at a loss what to do. So he sang of the young shepherd's realization that his life was, after all, the very best.

It was in this moment of indecision that the *paysan* turned the tables. Hard-pressed to keep his expression grave, he told of finding the young shepherd sitting on his perch, caught up in his contented thoughts while his sheep were being stolen by a smuggler.

The *paysan* had calculated well both the shepherd's fiery nature and his devotion to his sheep. In retort, the shepherd told of the fierce pursuit and accosting of the smuggler before the frontier was reached. In response, the *paysan* sang of the young shepherd and the smuggler in a frightful battle, belaboring each other with their staffs; and it looked as though the young shepherd was going to take a whipping and lose his sheep in the bargain. The shepherd could do nothing but defend his honor by telling of a glorious victory and the retrieving of the sheep.

Then the *paysan's* broad face broke out in a wreath of smiles. This time, his was the final stroke, and he proceeded to spring the trap. He sang of the *paysan's* flight from the noise and blood of battle, his disillusionment with the life of a shepherd, and of his return to his home, where a worried wife and children greeted him with loving arms and kindness.

So the second round had gone to the *paysan*. His champions whacked away at his strong back, and even his detractors were forced to shake their heads in admiration at the way he had turned the trick. The shepherd made an exaggerated bow, but because this was a serious business with him, his face showed no humor whatsoever. The *paysan* acknowledged the gesture with a mock bow of his own. His was a character that reveled in this combat of song.

In the third round the exchange was couplet for couplet, and without pause. The metered bursts were hurled back and forth. It was like a furious argument in which the arguers had to confine what they said to two lines, and rhyme them.

And as in a furious argument, it was here that their strengths and weaknesses were laid bare. There were impassioned words by the shepherd, whose nature was passionate, and there was humor and satire by the *paysan*, who refused to take anything seriously. They threw out challenges, assailed each other's positions, and matched barb for barb, but always short of insult, because an insult cannot be forgiven among the Basques.

When it was over, a new kind of argument began, this time among the villagers. They compared choice quatrains and couplets and argued over the quality of the improvising. When my cousin and I left, I asked him who had won.

"That matters little," he said. "If what they sang was important and beautiful enough, it will be remembered and sung again. If what they sang was unimportant," he shrugged, "it was at least a diversion for a rainy night."

The Healer

Until now, the healer had been allowed to live these many years without bother from anyone. But times are changing, and there are people in the village who claim that such primitive practices must be done away with.

The healer is the seventh son in a family of seven sons, and he is called in Basque *jainko-ttipi*, which is to say *little god*. It is said he was born with a tiny black cross on his tongue, but since no one seems to have seen it, I don't know if this is so.

There is nothing about him that is really very different from other men, except perhaps that one side of his face is a little lower than the other, so that it is like looking at a face in a broken mirror. And in the rare times he grins, it is a lopsided grin that reminds me of a saddened clown.

The healer is a shy man who lives alone in a little stone house that is always freshly whitewashed, and in the summer the open doorway is covered with a fringe of colored paper ribbons to keep the flies away. To earn his living, he does odd jobs in the village and helps on the farms in planting and harvest times.

From all that I have heard, he is an honest healer. He has had notable successes and notable failures, and there have been many times when he has told his people to go to a medical doctor for their sickness. He is not a mountebank like the woman I have heard of who has made much money selling potions and magic powders. What payment he gets is in gifts of tobacco and wine and poultry, and sometimes, a lamb.

Despite all this, he has been informed against. And not long ago, the government authorities came to the village and told him he would be put in jail if he did not stop. The healer has received no one since, because he is terrified at the thought of jail.

In the beginning there were those who were pleased. But now, they are not so sure.

Unknown to nearly everyone, a beloved old man of the village had been going to the healer. He went because the doctors had not been able to do anything for his asthma. He was to make twenty-two visits, and he had made twenty-one before the government authorities came. He has been failing badly ever since.

He will die soon.

The French Skier

She was Basque and he was French. She was the proprietress of a little Basque inn in the soft lowlands of the Pyrenees, and he was a teacher from a French school somewhere on the Atlantic coast.

He had stopped overnight at the little inn on his way to a skiing weekend in the high Pyrenees. When he came down in the morning to pay his bill, he was dressed in a brightly colored sweater and ski pants and after-ski boots.

She was a wizened woman with shrewd eyes and gray hair combed neatly back in a bun, and she sat on a high stool behind her desk, surrounded by account books and nail pegs on which many scraps of paper were impaled. She was an inquisitive old woman, and he was an outgoing man with an open way of talking.

"That's an unusual costume," she said, not unkindly.

"It's for skiing," he said, "You see, I'm going skiing."

She considered this for a moment. "And where do you do that?"

He considered this for a moment and decided she was not teasing him. "In the very high mountains where the snow is," he said.

"And is that far away?"

"Oh, no," he said. "About a day's drive from here."

"Well, that is far enough," she said. "Is there much snow there?"

"Oh, yes," he said. "It's very deep. About seven meters deep, I would say."

She drew her black shawl closer in an involuntary shiver. "I suppose it's cold, too."

"Oh, yes," he said. "It would have to be cold with all that snow. But that's part of skiing."

"I suppose so, " she said. She paused for a moment, and then decided to risk her pride. "And how do you do this skiing?"

He was patient as the schoolteacher he was, and explained with his hands. "Well, you take two long pieces of wood that are especially made for slipping over the snow, and you strap them on your feet. That way, you can slide over the snow."

She was intrigued. "That makes sense," she said. "It really does. But still, it must be difficult."

"Yes, it's difficult," he admitted frankly. "Until you learn how. And then it becomes easy."

"Well, that is the way with all things," she said. "But it must be dangerous, too."

"There are always injuries," he said a little boastfully. "You see, you go to the top of a hill, and then you put on your skis and slide down to the bottom of the hill. Naturally, you go very fast."

Now that her curiosity was satisfied, she sighed and smiled. "Well, that's very interesting," she said. "Indeed it is. But tell me one thing more. How much do they pay you to do that?"

A Peaceful People

It was one of those nights in winter when the wind changes suddenly to the south. After long weeks when the ground is covered with frost and breath freezes in the air, it is a disturbing wind that blows warm and troubles the blood. The Basques claim that it carries the undesirable passions of Spain and Africa. When the south wind blows, it is a night when anything can happen.

And sometimes it does.

Over a bottle of red wine in the tavern, the village scholar was discoursing to me. He has thought much, and what he has to say is not trivial. But he does not often have an audience for this thinking. The villagers do not like to be informed of why they act the way they do. They are what they are, and that is sufficient knowledge for them.

I like most the village scholar's epigrams. He has said to me such things as, "The Basques are true diplomats; they say first what they should have saved until last." And, "The reason why the Basques have survived the ages is that they have ignored their invaders; it is also the reason why they have learned so little."

I said to him that in my time in the country, I had seen only one incident of violence, and that I considered this remarkable. And he said that it was a point of conduct among the Basques to ignore what was not worth fighting about. "Because of this," he said, "we are considered a peaceful people."

While we were talking, the quiet of the village street was shattered by the exploding roar of motorcycles. At another table across the room, three men singing dropped their voices momentarily in recognition. And at the bar, the tavern keeper who had been listening to the singing shook his head as though regretting he had stayed open a little too late.

The young men who came in were of the type that are called *blousons noirs*. One sees them often in the big coastal cities, with long hair and high-heeled boots and the black leather jackets from which they take their name. They stepped through the doorway and looked about the tavern with wary insolence, as dramatic as if they were playing a role. Their expectant faces and tightly strung movements were not part of a role, however. Anyone could see they were bent on trouble.

"What do you have to drink?" said their leader. He was tall, with a long-boned face and bad teeth.

"What do you prefer?"

"Something you don't have."

"What is that?" the tavern keeper said imperturbably.

"Whiskey."

The tavern keeper reached under the bar and came up with a whiskey bottle and three glasses. He did not fill the glasses, but stood waiting with his hand on the bottle. When the money had been put down on the bar, he filled the glasses, took the money, and returned the change.

The *blouson noir* with the long-boned face repaid the compliment. "I see the peasants are finally developing taste."

My friend was sitting with his back to the *blousons noirs*. "Do you want to leave?" he said.

I shook my head.

"You are reacting like an American. They are nothing. Ignore them."

The villagers at the other table had stopped singing and were talking in Basque. One of the *blousons noirs* said to them, "What kind of language is that?" When no one answered him, he said, "You should speak in a civilized language."

The villagers said nothing, but regarded him with closed-down faces.

Finding no luck there, I suppose the *blousons noirs* would have confronted my friend and me next. "I warn you for your own good," my friend whispered. "Those are not peppermint sticks they are carrying inside their jackets."

The *blouson noir* with the long-boned face had

gone to the window to look outside. What he saw there made him whip open the door. "Keep your hands off our machines!" he shouted.

A voice from outside said, "I was only looking."

"Happily for you," the *blouson noir* said.

A *paysan* came into the tavern. Murmuring a greeting to the room, he went to the end of the bar. From his manner, it was plain to see that he had already dismissed the incident from his mind.

I recognized this man. Once when I had been standing beside my car on a country lane, he had come down the mountain with a great sack of grain balanced on his shoulder. He was a giant with a simple, open face, red hair that peeped out from under his beret, and a chest that sprang awesomely from where his neck met his body.

He had stopped to ask questions about the car—what country it had come from, what its horsepower was, how much fuel it consumed, and how much it cost. I had stood watching him in fascination. For the full half-hour we talked, he did not even bother to lower his crushing burden. When his curiosity was satisfied, he went on his way as effortlessly as if he had been carrying a sack of feathers.

If the *blousons noirs* were having second thoughts, I could not have blamed them. They were arguing in conspiratorial tones, glancing from time to time at the *paysan*. Drinking his wine and visiting with the tavern keeper, the *paysan* seemed unaware of their existence. But when the tavern keeper left him to fill the whiskey glasses again, the *paysan* turned and regarded the *blousons noirs* with frank curiosity.

That decided the long-faced leader.

"What do you find so interesting?"

"You," the *paysan* said pleasantly.

The *blouson noir* was stung. "Do you find something amusing in us?"

The *paysan* was nonplussed. "Why do you want to make an argument?" he said. "There is nothing to argue about."

"I asked you a question," the *blouson noir* said. "Do you find something amusing in us?"

"It's a question that deserves no answer," the *paysan* said wearily. "Now, will you leave me alone?"

"Of course I will leave you alone," the *blouson noir* said. He shrugged and made a motion as if to turn away. Then wheeling, he struck without warning.

The *paysan* was not hurt. The *blouson noir* would have needed an axe to accomplish that. But the *paysan* was so astounded that one would have thought he had never been struck in his life. Putting his elbows on the bar, he hunched his shoulders and bowed his head between them like a sorrowing child.

The sound of bone against flesh had brought the three villagers and us to our feet. My friend jammed in the cork and grasped our bottle by its neck.

The *blousons noirs* had backed up against the bar with their hands inside their jackets. The tavern keeper was shouting at us in Basque, "Sit down! I am calling the gendarmes."

None of us will ever be sure what would have happened if a huge drop of blood had not dripped from the *paysan*'s nose onto the bar. He looked at it wonderingly, and then raised his hand to his nose. It came away red with blood. The *paysan* stared at his hand for a moment, and then he went berserk.

As methodic as the savagery was, it was accomplished in a matter of seconds. The *blouson noir* with the long face had only time to turn his head before he was gathered up in the *paysan*'s arms. There was a rush of expelled air and the crack of bones. When the *paysan* opened his arms, the *blouson noir* flopped to the floor like a rag doll.

Of his two companions, only one remained faithful. It was a futile gesture, even if he did have a knife in his hand. The *paysan* caught his wrist and jerked, and the *blouson noir*'s arm was suddenly much longer than it had been before. He screamed once and fainted.

Casting his head about like a bull, the *paysan* looked around questioningly for the third man. The roar of a motorcycle in the street provided him with an answer. He glanced down once at the evidence of his mayhem, shook his head in disgust with himself, and went out.

When he was gone, the tavern keeper unhurriedly dragged the *blousons noirs* out onto the sidewalk, phoned the police with instructions where they could be found, and then closed down the bar.

I have never discussed the incident with my friend, the village scholar. If I had, he would have blamed what happened on the undesirable passions of the south wind.

Homecoming

There was a funeral in the village today that should not have been.

It was that of an old man who had come home from America to spend his last years in ease. His was an expectation that was fully earned and never realized. The old man came home only two weeks ago.

There are those who remember how it was with him when he left fifty years before. He had been a boy from a poor property and a poorer family that could not afford to feed him. From the age of ten, he had been hired out as a shepherd and sent to the mountains.

Even there, he had not fared much better in matters of nurture and clothing. His food was corn cakes and the skim milk that was residue from the cheeses he made in the shepherds' huts. He rarely had meat, he was fortunate if he had coffee once a year, and he had never tasted wine. In summer he went barefoot, and in winter he wore wooden shoes stuffed with fern that went for stockings.

When he was eighteen he exchanged one form of servitude for another and went to America as a sheepherder. In this, he could count on being something like an indentured servant having to work at least a year to repay the American sheep owner for the price of his passage.

The rest of it, I knew better than the villagers. My childhood in America had been filled with sheepherders' stories of years of loneliness and winter blizzards and the burning desert sun.

But this old man seemed not to have been affected by all of that. When a boyhood friend went to see him on his sickbed, the old man mentioned only the kindness of the sheep owner who had hired him. When he had arrived in America, the sheep owner had given him sturdy Levi's and warm boots and a heavy sheep-lined coat. And in the camps, he had been provided with more varieties of canned foods than he had ever known, and of all things, as much coffee and wine as his tastes dictated. After that, he had never considered his sheepherder's life a privation. He had been born to worse.

And then, two months ago, the sheep owner died, and the old man decided to go home.

The property where he had lived as a boy was still in the family, but the only ones left now were his widowed sister and her three sons. She was a good woman, but her husband had been lazy. The three sons took from the same stock as the father. The property was run down, the sons were notorious for their shiftlessness, and nobody had any use for them.

The old man had come home unannounced. He had taken the old rickety train from the seacoast to the mountains, and in the village he had made only two stops. The first was at the little bank, where he had deposited an immense dollar draft that represented fifty years of savings in America.

The second stop was at a little clothing store where he exchanged his American hat for a beret. When the proprietor asked him why, the old man said, "I have left America behind me. I want to go home the way I went from this country."

Though it was winter, the old man had on only a suit. The proprietor had asked him if he wanted to buy a coat, but the old man had said, "Oh, I'm used to the cold. After where I've been, this kind of weather can't bother me."

The proprietor recalled that the old man's destination was some distance from the village. He told the old man, "There's a taxi of sorts here now. For a few francs it will take you right to your home. Night is falling, you know."

I suspect the old man had still not crossed the bridge from his boyhood, so that to take a taxi now would have seemed an incomprehensible thing to do. He waved the offer aside. "It's only a little way, and God knows I am used to walking."

The old man had not adjusted to other things, either. By the time he reached the outskirts of the village, the snow came. It was a kind of snow he had become unaccustomed to, wet and heavy and falling through humid skies. In the hour that it took him to walk to his home, he was soaked to the skin and shivering violently from the dampness.

His sister received him with tears of astonishment and love, and put him to bed in an icy room. It was all the house had to offer. His nephews received him with disdain for his bedraggled appearance after having been in America so long. They probably expected him to come home in a Cadillac, as others before him had done. It was only when he was dying of pneumonia and told them of money in the bank, and they had verified it, that they changed their tune. After that, there was not enough they could do for him.

Penicillin and a warm room could have saved the old man, but it is doubtful whether his sister or his nephews had ever heard of such medicine. By the time they called the doctor, it was much too late for anything to help the old man.

I watched the cortege go by today. The old man's sister and his boyhood friends were sincere in their mourning. His nephews made a show of grieving, but there was already an air of arrogance about them that they never possessed before.

The villagers are certain of one thing. Though the old man never had a chance to enjoy his money, his nephews will.

Theater
of Restraint

They were both players of reputation, but they had never met on the handball court. This in itself was unusual, since there are not many *pilotaris* who play for money in that circuit of Basque villages. But

I suppose the old player was careful to avoid meeting the young ones whenever he could, because he had more to lose.

The old player had done pretty well with his handball, at that. With the money he made, he had bought a restaurant on the seacoast against the day when his name would not be in demand. The restaurant was so successful that he really had no need to play handball anymore.

The old player had once been blond, but his hair was beginning to thin and there was much gray in it. He had fair skin and eyes, a finely bridged nose, and the mutilated hands of a veteran *pilotari*. Age and the restaurant had given him an air of detachment and a beginning paunch. The young player had none of these problems. He was a carpenter's apprentice, and he was black haired and hungry for fame.

They had emerged together from the dressing room and descended into the well of concrete that was the handball court. At one end of the court, on floor level, there was a polite gallery protected with wire, and both the old player and the young player paused here before going out to warm up their hands. They carefully avoided glancing upward to the topmost gallery, which was a single row of benches flanking the long court.

This was the fearful gallery, lined with the Basque men of the village. With their black berets and beaked noses and black coats, they resembled a congregation of buzzards sitting in judgment.

Both *pilotaris* had on white shirts and white pants, and their waists were encircled by sashes — one with red and the other with blue. That much was tradition. The only departure was that the white, rope-soled sandals of other days had given way to tennis shoes.

Before they went out onto the court, the old player reached into his pocket and took out a roll of tape. Turning so that the fearful gallery could see what he was doing, he began to tape two of his mangled fingers together. The young player stood sympathetically by.

While he was performing the operation, the old player shrugged and said in a brave voice, "It is nothing. Merely one of the handicaps that an old *pilotari* comes to expect."

"Yes, and I won't escape them, either," the young player said loudly, "if I am fortunate enough to become the great *pilotari* that this man is." And the old player and the spectators nodded approvingly. Nobody remarked that the taping could have been performed more conveniently in the dressing room.

The fearful gallery came a little to life when the dry whack of the doghide ball against the far wall began to echo through the silent court. There was a low murmur of conversation, a pointing of fingers at some good exchange, and a cautious beginning of the betting.

The temper of the match, if not the outcome, was shown in the warm-up. The young player was agile and his strength lay in his speed and the power of his smashes. He was not in the least concerned with any lack of finesse. With his strength and speed, he fully intended to beat the old player down to the ground. The old player moved very little during the warm-up. He was carefully sounding the weaknesses of the young player.

After the warm-up had ended and the match was to begin, the old player sauntered to the polite gallery. He shook his head sadly. "I will never be able to do it. He has got the youth and the speed. My muscles are asleep."

When he was done, the young player came to the polite gallery and said, "Can you believe it? That man is forty-nine years old, and he's stronger than I am." And the gallery agreed with each one in turn.

For a while after the match began, it seemed that the old player had been closer to the truth. It was not that he had already given up, because he fought fiercely for each point. It was that the young player had won the toss for the first serve, and had not let go of that advantage. He served murderously, running to the service line with powerful shoulders hunched over and smashing the ball so that its rebound carried in a high arc all the way to the back wall. The old player returned it as best he could, but his best did not seem to be enough.

At the end of each exchange, the young player threw himself flat on the floor as if he had fainted and lay there as if he could never get back on his feet again.

The old player returned faithfully to the polite gallery and said, "What did I tell you? The old body is asleep. What a fool an old man is to think that he can compete with youth." And another time, "No, I've lost this one. He is too much for me. I should have retired in dignity when I had the chance."

Then, when the serve changed, the match changed, too. The old player opened his bag of tricks—changing pace with every shot, banking his serves so that they caromed from the front wall to the side wall, mixing hard drives with soft kills.

At the end of these exchanges, it was the young player who came to the polite gallery. He leaned on it with sweat pouring from his face and his chest heaving. "What he knows, I will never learn in a lifetime. Did you note the cleverness of that last shot?" And another time, "I am erratic. I don't have the temperament for this game. I have deceived myself into believing that I could ever be a *pilotari*." The young player's hands were swollen to twice their size and they were turning purple, but he made no mention of that.

The fearful gallery was merciless. They taunted the old player about his belly and his reluctance to run after a shot, and they tried to infuriate the young player by throwing a coin down to the floor as value for his performance. The young player picked up the coin, and bowing graciously, gave it to the umpire as if to make up for a dismal match. Even the fearful gallery applauded him for that.

In the matter of sport, it was not a dismal match. Before it was over, the contest had gone point for point all the way to sixty points, and no one could have been let down by that.

But in the matter of conduct, the match turned out badly. The last rally was the fiercest of the whole contest. When it was over and the young player had won, he could not contain himself but leaped straight into the air with an arrogant shout of victory.

The fearful gallery did not applaud him, and the old player did not shake his hand. The young player left the court with his head hanging. He had much to learn, including the proper demeanor of winning.

Maïtia

Outside the tall hedge that separates our house from the lane, Maïtia is waiting. He does not look at the house, but stands with his hands stuffed into his pockets and pretends to stare at the ground. He waits unannounced, like a black cloud in the sunlight of the lane.

Maïtia is a boy of the village, and he is my son's friend. He comes often to the house, but never to the door. In the manner of the country, he knows that sooner or later he will be noticed.

Such opposites I have never seen. My son is sturdy and fair-haired. Maïtia is thin as a razor and dark, and as shy as a wild animal. He has never spoken to me, and when I happen upon him in the village he will cross the street to avoid me or turn away quickly and go back in the direction from which he was coming.

In school, my son loves his studies, and in his American way wonders often of the future. Maïtia despises school, and though he has a good mind, is merely filling out his time until he can be free of studies. My son has told me that they have argued about this, but Maïtia thinks him foolish. He does not believe in horizons beyond the confines of the village.

When it comes to courting, Maïtia insists that they meet their sweethearts in the forest. If my son chooses to walk with his girl through the village streets, he must do so alone. Maïtia will not walk with a girl in the village. He wants no reins on him that people can point to.

Only in contest does Maïtia come outside of himself. And then he is truly like an animal, quick and with astonishing strength, the world outside forgotten. Whether it is jai alai or handball, his concentration is so perfect that wild low cries escape from him when he leaps for the ball. But always, he and my son must be on opposite sides.

The other day, I saw them fight. It began with horseplay, but in a little while, they were at it in earnest. It was a fight to see. Maïtia was the fiercest, but my son does not like to lose, either. When it was over, and Maïtia had been pinned, he ran off like a wounded deer.

He is back today, and the fight seems to be forgotten. They are sitting on the distant curb, speaking only rarely and not looking at each other. Maïtia is playing with a rock and my son is pulling kernels out of a stem of wheat.

In a little while, they will get up and walk down the lane toward the village, like sunlight and shadow walking together in the contradiction of friendship.

A Newborn Lamb

Today was market day in the village.

The men's livestock market began in the early morning, and the winding central street of the village was a scene of much confusion.

The *paysans* came down from their mountain properties with pigs and calves and lambs. The calves came on foot, with ropes around their necks and tails twisted firmly in their masters' hands. The lambs were bound by four feet, and they were carried upside down. The pigs rode in little mule-drawn carts, serene and comfortable on beds of straw.

Those *paysans* with calves to sell were in place under the ramparts of the old fortress, where there are wooden stalls. The carts bearing pigs were grouped together further along the ramparts. And the *paysans* with lambs were gathered across the street, under the protection of the plane trees. In a little while, the buyers from the coastal cities would arrive in their long smocks, appraising a pig with a glance here and pummeling a calf or a lamb there.

In the rainy morning, the *paysans* wore sombre coats of black and brown. Their boots were muddy, and their berets were pulled forward against the rain. Their faces were burned by cold and scraped clean from shaving. Little stubs of cigarettes were tucked into the corners of mouths, and a hundred wisps of smoke curled upward into the gray rain.

Among the *paysans* standing under the plane trees, I recognized my neighbor and went to talk to him. At first, I did not notice the lamb at his feet. But when I chanced to look down, I saw him. He had curly white wool and gracefully curving horns and the four black stockings by which I remembered him. He lay shivering on the wet cobblestones, and when I bent to touch him, I felt his heart fluttering in his throat like a bird's.

The reason I bent to touch him was that I had been in my neighbor's barn when this lamb was born. I had heard him speak for the first time, protesting his birth. But it had been hopeless dawn when he made his mewing cry. The barn in which he was born was cold and dark, and outside, the eastern sky was streaked with soot and the bare trees on the hillsides held fearful mysteries.

Then the sun had come up. And in an instant, the clouds were transformed into puffs of rose in a blue and fragile sky, and the branches of trees became cobwebs glistening with dew. When the sheep moved out to the green pasture, the lamb had gone, too. He had stood still with his legs planted uncertainly under him and felt the gentle warmth of the sun and stared with great round eyes at the beauty of the world.

April

Last night while the valley was black with sleep, a giant came and planted the forests.

They were not here yesterday and they were not here the morning before. Except once in passing, when the bare branches of a single tree made a shape like bat wings against the sky, I had forgotten their existence. In the long winter, they had sunk leafless into the brown and rusted landscape, and having died, were quickly forgotten.

Then suddenly this April morning the valley is filled with magic forests. They rest like crowns on the knolls and mantle the hillsides in a hundred shades of green. There are some with white blossoms like bridal wreaths in the green, and others whose fragrance goes to the head like wine.

When summer ends, the forests will die and I suppose I will forget them again.

Bells

From first light this morning, the air has been filled with the sound of a thousand bells.

It is a time of great occasion, because on this day in May, the sheep begin their long ascent from the valley floor to the peaks of the Pyrenees, there to graze upon the rich grass until snowfall.

All the country lanes have been crowded with tiny flocks, each starting from its farm at hours appointed by tradition. It is tradition, too, that every flock must pass through the village on its way to the high mountains.

The sheep are shining white from the spring rains and from the brushings they have received in the hectic week of preparation before. Their curling wool hangs down like a blanket almost to the ground. They have patrician noses and their gracefully curved horns have been decked with ribbons by the children. Each flock is distinguished from another by splashes of powdered paint, red and yellow and blue and orange, at different places on the white backs.

When they pass through the village, the leaders of the flock come first with staidly nodding heads and huge gourd-shaped bells that make a deep and hollow sound befitting their age. The lambs who frolic on the edges of the flock have collars shaped from green willow, and bells that make a tinkling sound.

At the heels of the sheep are the little shepherd dogs with quick movements and eyes that peep brightly from behind long fringes of hair.

And lastly come the shepherds, leading mules piled high with bedding and white sacks with provisions they cannot find on the mountain, wine and coffee and tobacco and sugar and salt.

The shepherds are clean-shaven for the occasion. Some are dressed in berets and suits, as if they were going to church. Others wear the costumes of times before, jerkins made from the pelts of lambs, woolen cloaks against the cold of the mountains, and legs bound up with leather thongs. Long black umbrellas with cane handles are hooked behind on the collars of suits and cloaks, and all of them carry a wooden staff worn smooth by the touch of their hands.

The shepherds walk as if they were in a parade, as indeed they are, because their flocks must bear the appraisal of the villagers who line the streets. The shepherds walk straight and proud, with the remote faces of men who have learned to live in solitude. They are not without their vanity, however, and the villagers' response to the quality and beauty of each flock is reflected in the shepherds' demeanor.

The procession has lasted until darkness. Now that it is over, the mood of the village has changed. In every country lane, in every house that touches upon

a meadow, in every dawn and sunset, the sound of
bells is gone.

The Little People

On the valley farms and in the high mountains,
I have asked my various families about the *laminak*,
the little people of the Basques.

My younger cousins laugh at me and parry my
questions. But the old women do not. They tell me
wondrous tales of how the *laminak* live in holes in
the deep forests and in caves on the mountain. They
recite as gospel the legends of treasure hordes in these
holes and caves, and of young girls blessed with for-
tune for their kindness to the little people.

But the stories I like best are of the *laminak* coming into a house in the dead of night, when the family is asleep. The *laminak* sweep the floors, dust the
lamps, and polish the copper and brass on the mantle.
But always, it seems, they manage to break something of value. This is not out of malice, but simply
an accident of their yearning to do good.

Afterwards, they weep in the night because they
have tried to attain the stature of human beings, and
have failed.

The Hairy God
of the Forest

My cousin addressed me, but the barb was directed at Erramun. "Now you will hear a shepherd's story about the hairy god of the forest," he said. "You will find it not unlike an old wives' tale."

With the hand that held the knife, Erranum lifted a morsel of bread and cheese to his mouth. The long blade formed an imperfect cross against the thin line of his lips, and then came away. There had been the slightest of tremors when the knife met his lips.

"Listen," Erramun said. "I personally do not hold with superstition. But there are others up here who will not venture into the forest at night."

Erramun's hut was long and narrow, with thick walls of little stones fitted neatly in place. Ages of smoke from the open firepit had turned these stones as black as the slates on the roof. There were no windows and the only exterior light came from the smoke shutter and a doorway so low that I had had to bend nearly double to pass through it.

Hams and bacons shrouded in white sacks hung from the great center beam that supported the roof. On one end of the hut, crude shelves held rows of cheeses that Erramun had made from the milk of the sheep. And on the other end, a bed made of poles rested against the wall. Rusted edges of bracken and coarse woolen blankets made up the rest of Erramun's bed.

A low fire was burning on the earthen floor beside the doorway, and outside, a white mist lay like a smothering blanket over the green mountain that is the crest of the Pyrenees. The mist had filled the protecting lees that held the stone huts of the shepherds.

I was content to watch the mist and listen to Erramun's story from the shelter of the hut. That afternoon, I had wandered away from Erramun and my cousin to explore the fringe of the forbidding forests below. The white mist had caught me, and in my groping return to the hut I had almost stepped off a precipice. They had been angry with me for wandering in the mist, and that had precipitated the shepherd's story.

"It is not my story, but that of my grandfather," shrugged Erramun. "You can make what you want out of it."

"I apologize to your grandfather," said my cousin. "We would be pleased to hear the tale."

The slight to his grandfather satisfied, Erramun began:

"When my grandfather was a boy, there was an old patriarch who was the law on this mountain. Not for thirty years and more had any of the shepherds challenged his authority. He was the one who judged all arguments. He was the one to whom the shepherds came with their grievances. He was the one who decided when a man's pasturage had been trespassed, which shepherd was mistreating his dogs, and who had started an argument in the first place. He was the one who heard the evidence and handed down judgment.

"Even though he was already old when my grandfather was young, the patriarch was a man of terrible size with great shoulders and longer arms than any of the other shepherds. But it was not this alone that made him ruler. He possessed a fierceness so far beyond the ordinary that it was said he carried the old blood.

"It was said that when he was young, life on this mountain was full of excitement. When he awakened in the morning too full of himself, he would step out of his stone hut and scream out the *irrintzina*. There were many who took up his challenge, and the mountain rang with the crash of wooden staffs.

"When all of his opponents had been defeated, it was natural that he should become the leader. Since there were no more battles to fight, he turned his strength to wisdom and justice, and in the end became the patriarch.

"There were grumblings, of course. But his justness over the years took the bitterness away from the punishments he laid down.

"There was one who remained bitter, however. He was a boy by the name of Balentin, who had committed the sin of thievery. This was unpardonable, even for a youth. By the patriarch's order, Balentin was beaten for his crime, one blow of a wooden staff from each shepherd on the mountain. The boy never forgot it.

"Nor did he forgive it. As he grew to manhood, his one desire was for vengeance. He was the rebel on the mountain, but he was not unclever about it. Because the patriarch was old, Balentin knew that he could not issue a challenge without risking intervention by the other shepherds. And so he set about disputing the patriarch's judgments and making insults that he knew would be carried back to the old man.

"The patriarch never revealed whether he saw through the young rebel. He bore the attacks as long as he could, but old age had not killed the fierceness that had once been so strong in him. One day in his anger, the patriarch warned Balentin that a beating awaited him if he kept on. It was not exactly a challenge, but Balentin was quick to make it one. In the presence of the other shepherds, Balentin said he could not accept the challenge because the patriarch was an old man. It was the final and greatest insult, and the patriarch insisted. After that, there was nothing the other shepherds could do to intervene.

"They met in the early morning in the hollow that lies in the center of these huts, where there is a single patch of level ground. The hillocks that surrounded the hollow were lined with shepherds, and my grandfather was one of them.

"The patriarch, out of the habit of his youth, had bound his forearms and calves with thongs of leather. He was still gaunt and great despite his years. But Balentin was an ox with legs and arms like trees, and he was young, and that made all the difference.

"When they came together the first time and locked their staffs, there was no doubt how it would end. My grandfather never forgot the sound of the old patriarch's wheezing, the whistle of Balentin's staff, and the crack of wood against bone. After each exchange, the patriarch grew weaker.

"Three times, Balentin could have walked away and declared himself winner. But there was too much hate in him. He kept the fight going until the patriarch was stretched out on the grass like a dead man. And then he brought his staff down like a club on the old man's head.

"Balentin was saved from his second common beating by one thing. When the shepherds came down the hill after him, they saw from his eyes that he was insane.

"In the few days of life that remained to the patriarch, the fire in his hut never went out. Each in his own turn, the shepherds ministered to him and tended to the milking and feeding of his sheep.

"The only one who did not come to the hut was Balentin. He was an outcast whom everyone avoided and who avoided everyone, keeping to his own hut and his own piece of ground.

"In that time, the shepherds were never certain whether the patriarch ever really came back to his senses. He lay for hours so still that the shepherds were hard put to find a sign of life in him. Then, when they were convinced he had died, the patriarch would suddenly awake and take nourishment and begin to talk.

"In the beginning, the shepherds were able to make some sense out of what he was saying. The things and the people he talked about were in the past, but not so long past that some of the shepherds could not remember. When he began telling them of men he could not have known on the mountain, they put it down to memory of stories told him in his childhood.

"But after that, there was nothing they could put his stories down to except the blow on his head. Not even in imagination had anyone ever conceived of such companions and such battles with strange beasts and unknown invaders.

"The worst was yet to come. The patriarch began telling them of a visitor who came to the stone hut each night in the darkness before dawn. Always it was the same story with only the smallest of changes. The patriarch told of wakening in the last hour of darkness to see a creature covered with hair crouching on his haunches beside the fire. The creature never spoke when the patriarch called out to him, but stared into the fire as if he were a man and the fireside was his own.

"Other times, the patriarch would cry out in his sleep for vengeance. That did not disturb the shepherds because they could at least understand his words. But when he began to speak in animal sounds they could not understand, they knew it was time to begin praying for his soul.

"On the night the patriarch died," said Erramun with a gesture of his hand, "a white mist such as you see out there came over the mountain. It was so thick that even at dawn, a man could not see his hand in front of his face.

"Then the sun came up, and the mist began to

burn away. When the air was clear, the shepherd whose hut lay nearest to that of Balentin noticed something. There was no smoke rising from Balentin's hut. His sheep were not in their paddock, but scattered over the slope. And there were many vultures circling in the open space beyond the precipice.

"The shepherd did not want to go to Balentin's hut, but finally decided nothing would be lost by it. What he found there was unexplainable. It was as though a great battle had been fought inside. The hut was torn to pieces. There was no sign of Balentin anywhere. The shepherd found only his dog, who was still shivering in his hiding place under the bed.

"Afterwards, the shepherd went to the precipice and looked over the edge. What he saw there answered the question of why so many vultures were flying around.

"That morning, the shepherds descended to the bottom of the abyss by a roundabout path, and recovered Balentin's body. Beside it was the carcass of a belled ewe, one of the leaders of the flock. It was clear then what had happened. The flock had broken out of its paddock during the night. Balentin had gone after them in the white mist and made the mistake of following the belled ewe over the precipice."

Erramun fell silent as though his story were ended. But it was clear that there was something else he wanted to say.

"What did the body look like when they found it?" my cousin asked.

"My grandfather said it was torn up very badly,"

said Erramun. "But what can you expect when a man has taken a fall from a precipice?"

"What about the condition of the hut?" I said. "Did you ask your grandfather about that?"

"Certainly," said Erramun. "The shepherds put it down to the fact that Balentin had, in an insane rage, wrecked his hut."

"No more than that?" I asked.

Erramun did not look at me when he answered. "Of course not," he said. "Who of them could have continued to live on this mountain if he believed otherwise?"

Victor's Horses

There was an auction of horses in the village today.

I wanted very badly to go, because there was a little mare that I intended to buy. I saw her a week ago, when the frontier guards brought a troop of Spanish horses through the middle of the village. They were contraband horses that Victor, one of the local smugglers, had tried to pass over the frontier by night. Most times, Victor is successful. But this time the frontier guards were lucky and they captured the horses.

Yesterday, the town crier announced that there would be a public auction of the contraband horses in the village.

I was helping my neighbor and his hired man in planting corn. As the sun rose higher in the sky, I asked my neighbor often what time it was getting to be. And finally he said, "Why are you so interested in the time?"

So I explained that there was to be an auction of contraband horses in the village, and that I wanted to buy a particular mare.

My neighbor's hired man was leaning over the sideboard of the old wooden cart, his beret tipped back and his straight hair falling down over his forehead. He is a man who speaks rarely, but this time he said, "Don't take the trouble."

"Why not?" I asked him.

"Because it would be a waste of time."

"It is a public auction, isn't it?"

"Oh, yes," he said. But the only public that will be there will be Victor the smuggler."

Thinking that I was beginning to understand, I said, "I am not really of this village, so I can go. Perhaps I may even outbid Victor on the mare."

"Most probably you will," the hired man said. "And of course you will take the mare to your house."

"Of course."

"And you will put her in your field?"

"Of course."

"And tomorrow morning, the mare will be gone."

"What do you mean?" I demanded. "Who will take her?"

"Victor the smuggler."

"But that would be stealing!"

"No, it would not be stealing," the hired man said. "She is Victor's horse."

I looked to my neighbor for support. "Now that that is over," he said, "shall we get back to work?"

The Monk

He had always wanted to be a monk. But monk he could not be because he was consumptive, and the rules of health are unyielding in monasteries.

So he went to live in a deserted stone cabin of one room and four walls. The cabin is high on the mountain and on the edge of the forest. There are no roads to the cabin. It is absolutely enclosed by tangled growths of bracken and bramble bushes.

The cabin is bare except for a pallet of straw and a table where he eats his meals and reads his missal and writes mystical poetry. It is said he eats no meat, but lives on vegetables from his little garden and walnuts and chestnuts and berries that he gathers in the forest. And it is also said that he goes barefoot in winter, when the ground is frozen.

He wears a makeshift robe of black cloth that is like a monk's, but not quite, because the large crucifix and the prayer beads are missing. Though his hair is clipped short, he does not pretend to the tonsure, either.

His only visitors are his family, who go occasionally to take him bread and salt and paper and pencils, and to remonstrate with him. He receives them warmly and talks to them of the thoughts he has arrived at in his solitude. He does not hate the world. He merely loves God. Monk he could not be, but monk he has become.

The House
of Arretalepho

In order to make the descent to the hamlet from their farm on the faraway mountain, they had to begin walking in the darkness. For the young, the task was easy. But for the old, like Chemarc, the descent through tangled forests and down narrow footpaths must have been torture.

The hamlet they came down to is in the high Basque country, where my father was born. It is a tiny cluster of weathered stone buildings grouped around a three-steepled church. The hamlet lies in a long narrow valley flanked on either side by sheer green mountains.

I met them where they had changed their shoes in an old barn that lies not far from the church. The barn is set aside for the people who live in the high mountains and must walk a long way to come to

Mass. This is a kindness that has been offered by the successions of the family who own the barn. Each Saturday, its floors are swept clean. And each Sunday, its walls are lined with neat rows of wooden shoes cracked with age, and the newer mode of rubber boots caked with the springtime mud of mountain paths.

Today was Easter Sunday, and therefore an occasion for joy. But for us, it was also the first anniversary of the death of my father's sister, and therefore an occasion for the ritual of mourning.

When I saw her last, she was an old, old woman with a seamed face and hair that never really turned white and a voice that boomed out of deep caverns. Her humor was indomitable. I remember once when we made the climb to her house on the faraway mountain and had seen a drowned chicken in the creek below the farm. When we told her and wondered how it had happened, she said, "There is nothing to wonder about. It's a common occurrence hereabouts. She lost her footing and broke her neck." My aunt lived to be nearly a hundred. One night a week, she went without sleep to wash the family's clothes in the icy creek below. The day before she died, she was planting corn on those impossible slopes.

The name of the house on the mountain where my aunt had lived was Arettalepho, and all of its members had made the descent. There was Josef, who was head of the household now, with the strain of fair hair and blue eyes that happens so often in these remote mountains. There was Gabrielle, the wife of old Chemarc, with the gray eyes and wedge face and amused detachment of the mother she had buried a year ago. There were cousins young and old. And finally, there was Chemarc, who was not of the valley but had married into the house of Arettalepho.

In the busy formality of embraces, I did not have a chance to notice that Chemarc had changed. My most vivid memory of him was when he had one of his times of boredom with the house on the mountain, and had come the long way down to the hamlet to drink and sing in the taverns. Refusing to adopt the changing dress of the village, he had worn the short pleated *chamarra* cloak and the wide black belt of times past. His gray moustache had been waxed until it flared like wings, and his fair skin glowed like a boy's. He had been bent on a good time, and he had one.

That had been when my aunt was oldest at the house of Arettalepho. But now she was dead, and Chemarc was the oldest. It was a happening that he had not counted on, and a distinction he did not welcome.

I was to find that out on our way from the barn to the church. Purposely, Chemarc had taken me by the elbow so that we could lag behind the others. The procession of women in black head scarves and black dresses and men in black berets and black suits passed us by.

The question was a demand. "How do you think I look?"

I glanced at him and saw that his blue eyes were swimmy with the water of old age. "I think you look fine."

"Why don't you tell the truth?" he said angrily.

Why should I? I said to myself. And to him I said, "What's the matter? Don't you feel well?"

He was instantly content. "No. I haven't been feeling at all well."

"Well, what is it? Do you have a sickness?"

"Of course not," he said. "I'm just too old. I've lived too long, and everybody in the family knows it."

In these matters, one must be careful. But they were my family, too. "Do they tell you that?"

"They don't have to. I can see it in their eyes."

"I think you're imagining things."

He might have said something angry, but at that moment, a defiant old man passed in front of us and went into the church. Chemarc tightened his grip on my elbow. "See that old man? He has ninety-three years, but he doesn't want to quit this life, either."

The rest of the family were waiting for us at the entrance to the church. I looked at them and could sense nothing of what Chemarc had been talking about. We touched hands, and in the Basque custom, separated at the entrance. The women went down to the individual prayer chairs in the nave of the church, and the men made their way up the creaky wooden stairway to the gallery above. The railings and the benches had been hewn out of oak, and the ridges in them had been worn smooth over the centuries by the touch of ten thousand hands.

The benches in the gallery were tiered to the ceiling, and filled with the Basque men of the high mountains. They are different here, taller and more solitary, and they smile rarely. Burned bronze from exposure, they looked as if they might have been carved out of the same unyielding wood as their surroundings. The quiet strength that filled the gallery had its effect upon Chemarc, and in a little while, his shoulders were as erect as they once had been.

Beneath us in the nave of the church knelt the women, indistinguishable from each other in their black dresses and the scarves that hooded their heads. In the embracing sombreness, only the altar stood out in contrast. Against the gloom, it was a backdrop of brilliant colors—golds and purples and reds. On the wall above the altar was a gray-haired God holding the world in His hands. He was not a God of easy compassion. Taking away His long hair and flowing robes, He would have fit well in the gallery of men's faces that looked down at Him.

Because it was Easter Sunday, it was a sung Mass. The priest's part was sung in the high, clear soprano of the women below, and the responses flowed back in the melodious thunder of the men's voices above. Chemarc seemed to profit from the singing, too. But then at a certain point, the man who was the lead singer in the gallery stood up and sang alone. It was a hymn from a funeral Mass, and Josef whispered to me. "This song is in respect to our loss. One soul gone on a journey, and one voice to accompany it."

I stole a glance at Chemarc. His back was bent again, and the tears were coursing down his face.

On the outskirts of the hamlet, there is an abandoned church and a neglected graveyard, and it was there we walked when Mass was done. The church is so tiny that twenty worshippers would have made it crowded. Its walls are very thick and made of little stones, and its roof of heavy black slate sags down ominously on weakening gray timbers.

The graveyard that lies in front of the church is also very tiny. It is enclosed by a crumbling wall of the same stones that made the church, and a rusted iron gate that shrieks when it is opened. The graveyard is so very old that there are more discoidal tombstones with sun symbols than Christian crosses. Centuries neglected, they lie overturned or lean in fantastic postures.

The tombstone of the house of Arettalepho still stands. It is there my father's sister and all the antecedents of the house are buried. The women gathered in the first circle around the grave, and men in the second circle, and the young behind.

Perhaps it would not have happened if the day had been in summer, and flowers blooming, and the earth warm and inviting. But instead, it was a cold and rainswept day, and wind whipped at the black dresses and black shawls of the women. The required rosary droned on, but it was muffled by the sound of the wind and the tremulous keening of Chemarc. He was not crying from sorrow. The note in his voice said fear of the grave.

The young were the first to give up, shifting in embarrassment and finally stealing out of the graveyard and down the hillside. The men were the next to go, shaking their heads in disapproval. Chemarc was left alone with the women. I think they would have liked to leave him, too. But being women, they did not.

Wedding Supper

They were married that afternoon in the village church. And afterwards, while their clans went on to the restaurant where the wedding supper was to be, the couple went alone to the cemetery.

In the manner of the Basques, they stood beside the tombstone that marked the common grave of his ancestors. In the full bloom of their youth—he with his shock of black hair and she with her gown of white silk—they stood among the stones and crosses and looked upon the cold gray place where one day they would lie together in death.

And afterwards, they went to the restaurant to preside over the wedding supper. But it was after the appointed rounds of toasts and the restraint of sharing table with strange company that the first mingling of the clans began.

When the men were gone to the bar, the old

women in their high black dresses and cameo broaches gathered in a corner of the banquet room to compete in the nodding game of ailments and tribulations, and to place each other in the categories by which they would forever be known. And in the bar, the men stood in their coarse black wool suits and white laundered shirts and black berets, all of them involved in the first testing of imposed kinship. His was a family of big men with heavy shoulders and arms and almost voluptuous faces with curved mouths and thickly lashed eyes. And hers was a clan of men slender as sticks, with long fleshless faces and fragile noses and blue eyes.

Some of them played at cards, and their talk probed around the edges of their play. And after the wine had begun to flow, there was singing of Basque songs. Men of one family would sing a verse, and men of the other family would answer in kind. But in this, too, there was the measuring.

Only the young tasted laughter at the wedding supper. And it was left to them to break the bonds of restraint in the mingling of the clans. Theirs was the laughing game of first revealings of family secrets and scandalous ancestors and daring jokes about the marriage bed. And when they tired of sitting, they leaped to their feet as if by a common signal and formed a serpentine line that swirled through the bar and out into the darkness of the village street. There, with snapping fingers and flying feet and piercing yells, they formed a circle that dipped and rose as if it were one being.

Their singing passage was the flame that brought
the first warm smiles of accepted kinship and min-
gled the clans in a way that neither the wedding
ceremony nor the portent of the graveyard had done.

Reunion of Three Poets

It could not really be called a reunion, since the
three poets had never met. But they had been ex-
changing poetry for so long that they fancied they
knew each other in the deepest sense. And so, they
insisted on calling it a reunion.

One was an aristocrat from Pamplona who wanted
to do away with all institutions, beginning with the
Church. Another was a monk from a mountain monastery who wrote about universal love. And the third
was a shopkeeper from the seacoast, a Basque racist
who felt that all Latin populations should be syste-
matically exterminated.

The three poets chose the village for their reunion
because its location was central to all of them. Even
if the villagers had been forewarned, they would not
have considered themselves to be highly honored.
They do not appreciate poets much here. To them,
it is a form of art left for those who are neither good
singers nor good dancers.

The restaurant where the three poets met is one that tourists do not find. It is an unmarked restaurant on an unlighted street. The reason it is unmarked is simply that its proprietor, Paulo, is not interested in more business.

The restaurant has a high bar where villagers can stand and drink and sing to their hearts' content. Or nearly so. Paulo does not care how much they stand and drink, but their singing must be worthy of the name, or Paulo will tell them so.

Scarred wooden tables set end to end share the same room with the bar. There are no tablecloths, and the menu is always the same—soup in one common tureen, salad with vinegar and oil, mutton and pork, an omelette with peppers, and French bread and cheese and wine.

In all things concerned with the restaurant, Paulo is an autocrat. A shining bald head, satanic eyebrows, and powerful arms give him the appearance that goes with the role. He brooks no nonsense from anyone except his wife, who in her turn is the autocrat of the kitchen.

Of the three poets, the shopkeeper from the seacoast was the first to arrive. He was the most nondescript of men, slight and drooping, and clad in a worn gray suit. Probably because he was shy, he wore dark glasses. His mouth was formed in such a way that the ends turned up when he spoke, so he seemed always to be smiling.

So quietly did the shopkeeper sidle through the front door that it was a while before we noticed him standing at the edge of the noise and smoke.

"You're looking for someone," said Paulo in French. He never asked questions, but stated everything as a fact.

The shopkeeper seemed to be taken aback by this approach. "I was to meet two friends here," he said timidly.

"You see them."

"I don't think I see them," the shopkeeper said. "But then, I have no way of telling."

Because of the dark glasses, Paulo made an honest mistake. "You are..." he began. "I mean, you're capable of seeing."

"Oh, yes. Perfectly."

Paulo's satanic brows narrowed until they met. "You're making fun of me," he roared.

The shopkeeper raised his small hands in protest. "I'm not. I assure you."

"You're a tourist!" Paulo said accusingly. "Someone told you about this place. Just tell me his name, and I'll settle with him."

The shopkeeper must have had a sudden inspiration. In Basque, he said, "The friends I'm to meet are my friends by letter only, so I have never seen them."

Paulo's hostility vanished. "Ah! You're Basque. You should have said so in the first place. But you didn't!"

The shopkeeper was quick to seize the advantage. "Would it be possible to have a table for dinner?"

"It means more work for me," Paulo said resignedly. "Nobody cares what I have to go through."

"I wonder if I could have a menu."

Paulo clapped himself on the chest. "I am the menu."

The shopkeeper stared at him in confusion. Then, divining Paulo's meaning, he said, "Could you tell me what the menu is?"

"It's the same as always."

The shopkeeper said helplessly, "Well, that's fine."

"You had better be certain it's fine," said Paulo. I don't stand for any criticism of my wife's cooking."

The villagers had been watching Paulo's bullying of the strange little man with quiet amusement. Now, they turned away. The subject of Paulo's wife's cooking was no novelty. There was a shout for drinks, and Paulo reluctantly surrendered his victim. The shopkeeper retreated to an empty table.

In the front door of Paulo's restaurant there was embedded a small pane of glass. Once, the glass was used for looking through. But many layers of tobacco smoke and grease had made it so opaque that everyone had forgotten it was there. The glass had survived the rough handling of the door by thousands of hands over many years. It did not, however, survive the entrance of the aristocrat from Pamplona.

At the precise moment the aristocrat made his appearance, there was the accident of an almost complete lull in the shouting and singing. The door to Paulo's restaurant was flung open with such force that it crashed against the inside wall. There was the sound of tinkling glass, and a figure swept commandingly into the room.

From throat to ankle, the aristocrat was shrouded in a billowing black cloak. On his head, there was a huge black beret. Between the beret and the cloak, there were intense black eyes set in a face so white that one would doubt it had ever seen the sun.

The aristocrat strode to the center of the bar. Throwing one side of the cloak over his shoulder, he announced, "I am the poet!"

Paulo's attention had been fixed on the forgotten pane of glass and the hole its absence had left in his front door. "You are the what?"

"I am the poet from Pamplona!" said the aristocrat. "Are you so ignorant in these villages that you don't know your own celebrities?"

"You broke my window!"

The aristocrat actually sneered at him. "Put it on the bill!" Whirling, his eyes swept the room. "Where are my colleagues?"

Among the villagers, it is happily agreed that Paulo met his match that night. For the first time in anyone's memory, he had begun to ask questions. "Who are your colleagues?" he said.

"Poets, of course. Do you think I would consort with *paysans*?"

Paulo said simply, "No." He considered a moment and then pointed at the shopkeeper sitting alone at a table. "Is he a colleague?"

The aristocrat followed the direction of Paulo's extended finger. "Him? Of course not. Obviously, he is a shopkeeper, and an unsuccessful one at that."

"But he is the only stranger here," said Paulo. He stalked from behind the bar and stood towering over the little man. "You are a poet," he said.

"Well, some think so," said the shopkeeper.

Paulo strode back triumphantly to the bar. "He is a poet!"

But the aristocrat was not to be put down. "Of course he is," he said. "He is in shabby disguise to protect his privacy. Any fool can see that."

Paulo stared confoundedly at the aristocrat, as though trying to make up his mind whether he had been insulted. Before he could make an argument out of it, the front door opened again. Paulo's eyebrows flew upwards. There was a monk in his establishment.

The row of villagers at the bar straightened with a jolt. A few berets were whipped away from heads, and there was a muttered chorus of, "Good evening, Father."

The monk closed the door gently. He was a man ascetically thin, with pink skin and dreamy blue eyes that did not seem to be making contact with worldly environment. He was dressed in a long black cassock with a frayed collar.

Because he was the only man at the bar who could have been expecting a monk, the aristocrat was at the door with one swirl of his cloak. "I would have recognized you anywhere," he said. "Come! Let us meet our colleague. He is in disguise."

The monk smiled benignly and allowed himself to be led to the table where the shopkeeper waited. "The best vermouth you have," the aristocrat called out to Paulo. "And then you can begin serving dinner."

The shopkeeper stood up, one drooping hand extended for handshakes. The monk took it eagerly and the aristocrat took it with clear reluctance, as though he had begun to suspect that the shopkeeper was not in disguise, after all.

The three poets sat down and regarded each other. The monk, for whom any experience outside the monastery must have been rare, kept repeating, "How very pleasant." The aristocrat said passionately, "What an historic moment! This place will become a shrine." The shopkeeper said nothing at all.

"To poetry!" said the aristocrat when the vermouth was served. They clinked their glasses and drank, and then stared at each other wordlessly.

The aristocrat broke the silence. There was a note of desperation in his voice. "If only I had your gift," he said to the shopkeeper. "My muse is so inadequate."

The shopkeeper replied with his unfortunate smile, "It's not so much a question of gift as it is of hard work and sacrifice."

The aristocrat reacted as though he had been stung. "That is a clever disguise," he said with an unsteady voice. "No one could possibly suspect you of being a poet."

"It is no disguise," said the shopkeeper. "You see, I am an unsuccessful shopkeeper."

"Well, that is unfortunate," said the aristocrat with the malice of a great cat.

"Why should a poet worry about dress?" said the shopkeeper. "Does that make him a better poet?"

"A poet has a duty to be different," said the aristocrat. "He should not be mistaken for a..."

"A shopkeeper?"

"Well, something of the sort."

"I have found that those who affect bohemian garb and beards are usually failures as artists," said the shopkeeper.

"Or else they are aristocrats."

"I thought you might be of the aristocracy," said the shopkeeper. "May I be so bold as to ask your full name?"

The aristocrat pronounced the great names of his lineage.

"Gonzales?" said the shopkeeper.

"My grandmother's family name," said the aristocrat.

"But then you are not pure Basque," said the shopkeeper. "How unfortunate."

The aristocrat was not smiling anymore. "Why unfortunate?"

The shopkeeper threw up his hands. "When I wrote that the Latin bloods must be exterminated to purify the world, you agreed the point was well taken."

"That was poetry."

"Don't you believe in what you write?"

"But you are asking me to sign my grandmother's death warrant," the aristocrat said.

"You must accept that," said the shopkeeper. "The idea is bigger than your grandmother."

The monk had been following the conversation with a vague smile. When the aristocrat half rose from the table, the monk said in alarm, "Come, my dears. We must not let little differences mar this great moment."

There was silence until the soup was served. Then the shopkeeper said, "Tell me, father. In the embracing love you write about, does it extend to those who would destroy the Church, such as our colleague from Pamplona?"

"How can there be love if it does not embrace both friend and foe?" said the monk sweetly.

The aristocrat had the good grace not to laugh, and the shopkeeper looked chastized. "My apologies," he said to the aristocrat.

"Accepted," said the aristocrat with a bow.

Beaming with pleasure at the reconciliation, the monk ventured a small joke about his Father Superior. Both his companions laughed merrily, and the shopkeeper told of a friend of his who had written a letter to the Pope informing him that the bishop of the Basque provinces was not a Christian. Nobody seemed to notice that the monk did not laugh.

"I have a friend who has surpassed that," said the aristocrat. "He is convinced the Pope is more Christian than Catholic, and he prays every morning for the Pope's conversion."

The monk rose to his feet. Holding the soup tureen in both his hands, he said in a loud voice, "If I hear the good name of our men of honor in the Church soiled once more, I will break this over your heads!"

The aristocrat was so surprised that he sat back with his mouth agape. The shopkeeper had the bad judgment to say, "But you made the first joke."

The soup tureen descended and the shopkeeper slid gently under the table. The aristocrat cried out in horror, and the soup tureen came down again. This time, it broke.

The monk surveyed the damage he had wrought, halted Paulo's advance with one baleful glance, and took his leave. When they had recovered, the aristocrat and the shopkeeper also took their leave, soup-splattered and singly and without a word of goodbye to each other.

There have been no important reunions of poets in the Basque country for some time. Rumor has it that the three poets do not communicate with each other anymore, that the shopkeeper has become anti-clerical, the monk has confined his theories of love to members of the cloth, and the aristocrat has become a traditionalist.

There has also been a change in Paulo. He still does not welcome new business, but his attitude toward the occasional tourist who stumbles upon his restaurant is different. Paulo will serve him now without complaint, provided he answers a certain question satisfactorily.

Paulo has found there are more dangerous things than tourists in this world.

Mornings
in Spring

When I awake on summer mornings, it is to the sound of cocks crowing in near and distant farmyards and the ringing of the church bell in the village below. The air that comes in through the open windows is sweet with perfume and as soft as a child's caress.

On winter mornings, the cocks still crow and the church bell still rings, but the windows are shuttered and the sounds are dim and melancholy. The rain beats down on a dreary landscape and patters against the heavy wooden shutters.

But I like best the mornings in spring when the mists fill the valley like a white sea, obscuring the village and clothing the sounds of cocks and church bells with softness. When the sun comes up, the mists rise like a lifting veil to reveal the wonder of green mountains and a white village gleaming with wetness.

A Noble House

He was a youth of princely bearing and she was a girl of extraordinary beauty. He was of a noble house, a grand old chateau with towers and gracious gardens. She was the daughter of a gardener to the noble house, and she lived in a house in the village that matched her father's station.

The youth was dressed always in immaculate linen and fine wools, and he bore himself with the air of one whose hands had never known work. Because his schooling in Paris was not yet done, he came to live in the chateau only on vacations. But one day, it would be his duty to come back and govern the estate.

If the old story is to be believed, it had not always been so with this noble family. The boy's forefather had been a son of the soil, but he had so distinguished himself as a soldier that he became a marshal under Napoleon. In an invasion of Spain, the marshal had both French and Basque troops serving under him. To his French soldiers, he had passed the order that they were to make war like gentlemen. There would be no raping, no pillaging, and above all—no looting. To his Basque troops, he had said in their own language: "Take everything of value that you can lay your hands on. But remember, a third of what you take goes to your marshal." It was out of this booty that the noble house was founded.

I saw the youth and the girl together at a village fair on Midsummer Night. It was by chance. I had been coming down from the mountain and had met them strolling hand in hand into the forest.

I could not help noticing them later, when the young of the village were leaping through the flames of huge bonfires to test their courage. But they were not together anymore. The youth moved aloofly through the throng of people, and the girl was watching him. Her golden head was pensively bent as if to conceal the direction of her gaze, but her eyes followed his every movement.

"They are truly in love," I said to my companion who had told me the story of the noble house.

"Yes, they are in love."

"Will they marry?"

"Of course not," he said. "You Americans have such curious ideas. What has she to offer him?"

No Crossroads for Agustin

The vicar came from a large family on a farm property that could not hope to support all its offspring. This is not uncommon in the mountains of the Basque country, where nights are long and distractions few, and tampering with the course of nature is still a matter for the confessional.

By that late institution known as the Napoleonic code, the vicar could have claimed a share of property on the death of his parents. But in the mountain farms, tradition is a hundred times older and stronger than the law, and property passes to first son or daughter as it has for generations uncounted.

The rest of the children fare as best they can. The daughters marry into other properties or become nuns and servants. The old Basque code for the sons also goes unchallenged—one to the church, one as village artisan, and the rest to the Americas.

I suspect the security of priesthood compared to the unknown of foreign lands had something to do with the vicar's decision. But there are those in the village who say that he was the one who should have gone to the Americas. Some even go so far as to say it would have been better if he were an unvirtuous priest.

The vicar was slight and dark and quick of movement, and there was no denying that he was a sensuous man. Without a doubt, he was attracted to women. At the sidewalk cafes in summer, where he sometimes drank with village men, he tried to avert his eyes from the girls passing by in the street. He was not very successful.

There was one girl in particular whose presence he seemed to sense without raising his head. There was reason for it, because Panchika was something out of the ordinary. She had flaming red hair and milk-white skin, and no dress that her pious mother made her wear could hope to conceal the rising breasts and flaring hips. Until the evening before the incident of which I write, she did not suspect that her daughter was anything but a decent girl. The boys in the village could have informed her otherwise, but such confidences are not for old ears.

Fortunately for the parish, the doyen, who was the head priest, was an understanding man. By that, I mean that he did not deceive himself about the church's control over the failings of the flesh. It was a losing contest at best.

In body, the doyen was a small man with gray hair and fair skin and a nose of unbelievable fragility. In spirit, he had shrewdness in his eyes and a wise and humorous mouth. He reminded me of a good poker player. And indeed he rarely missed a Sunday afternoon of playing cards with the men in one of the village inns.

The doyen was in other ways a popular man, especially at confessions on Saturday night. The line to the doyen's confessional was always long and well sprinkled with the youth of the village, while the vicar's line consisted mostly of old women and little children who had little to risk.

This matter of risk was something to be considered because the vicar was not above hinting obliquely at the sins of the village in his sermons at Sunday Mass. This he did under the umbrella of priestly despair with his flock. His performance was convincing enough to fool the old, but the young are gifted in seeing through such fabric. They heard only the revealing and both feared and hated him for it.

Unhappily for them, there were times when a deathbed visit to an outlying farm or a trip to another village prevented the doyen from hearing confessions on Saturday night. These were times of terror for those who had something valid to confess. Some went through it anyway, because the force of ritual was too strong for them to break. The brave and the very guilty risked the private wrath of parents and the public wrath of the vicar by missing both Saturday confession and Sunday communion. Their only consolation was in the fact they would have been in worse trouble if the vicar knew all.

Panchika had been among those who chose simply to miss confession. But on this occasion, everything conspired against her. The doyen was absent. She had something of import to confess. The approaching Sunday was her feast day and there was no way on earth Panchika could avoid taking communion.

On that Saturday evening, she knelt for a long time in the cold gloom of the church. So long, in fact, that she was the last to make confession. Afterwards, it would have been hard to say who emerged from the ordeal more shaken, Panchika or the vicar. She was trembling when she knelt to say her penance.

When the vicar came out of the confessional, he was like a man demented. There was a cluster of old women who had been waiting to talk to him, but he brushed past them as if they did not exist and fled up the dark center aisle.

No one except Panchika could have anticipated what he was about to do. That was probably the reason why she remained in the church so long. The old women merely thought Panchika had been given a penance of rosaries unequaled in memory.

When finally she went home, it was to a frightful scene. The vicar had been there and left. But in the time he was there, he had destroyed the household. Panchika's mother had collapsed on her bed, and her father was waiting with a heavy razor strop in his hand. He did not have much of a chance to use it, however, because Panchika ran screaming into the night.

There is a little inn of doubtful reputation between the outskirts of the village and the Spanish frontier. It does not do much of a business in the wintertime, but when the French tourists come with their mistresses in the summer, the inn does very well.

On this midwinter night, the only guest in the inn was young Agustin, who was the son of a smuggler. Agustin had come over the Pyrenean pass from Spain at an hour early enough to reach his family home in the village. But he did not have the least desire to do so.

Agustin was what is known in argot as a *maquino*, which is to say the middleman between his father and the merchants who bought his father's contraband. It was a necessary profession and one that his father could not have been expected to perform. The success of any smuggler demands that he keep his distance from his respectable counterparts.

The role of *maquino* is lucrative, but it can also be discouraging. Agustin seemed always to be caught between two fires. Either the merchant who bought the contraband went away convinced that the price was too high, or Agustin's father was convinced that the price was not high enough.

This had been one of those days when Agustin guessed that the fire from his father's side was the one to worry about. And so he had abandoned the idea of a confrontation until the old smuggler had had a good night's sleep.

Besides *maquino*, there was another name by which Agustin was known. It was that of *garçon des fêtes*, which is a playboy. This was one name that did not offend him in the least, and he did his very best to live up to everything the name meant.

Apart from his dark good looks and brilliant smile in a country where teeth are often neglected, Agustin had a bullying set to his mouth that reminded one of a stubborn little boy. This pout combined with the judging eyes that came from being a *maquino* seemed to work powerfully in the business of conquest.

Being the son of a wealthy smuggler was no handicap when it came to acting out the role of playboy. For one thing, Agustin had a car, and this made him mobile. He was not bound to the village for his amusements. In the times when he was not working, he was a familiar figure in the discotheques of Biarritz on the Basque coast.

On this Saturday night, Agustin realized almost too late that the ambience of Biarritz might be exactly what he needed to forget his troubles. He had eaten alone in the dining room of the little inn, and afterwards he had ordered another bottle of wine and shared it with the innkeeper. When that durable soul had gotten weary of hearing about the trials of being a *maquino*, he went to bed. Since Agustin was a young man of the village, the innkeeper simply gave him a key to the front door and told him to lock up if he decided to go to Biarritz.

Agustin went up to his room, turned up the gas heater against the cold, and then as quickly abandoned the idea of bed. Going downstairs, he roared off toward the village, which he had to pass through on his way to Biarritz.

Somewhere on the darkened streets of the village, he found Panchika. Afraid to go home and too proud to ask for refuge in the house of a friend, she was walking in the cold trying to figure out what to do with the long night, and with her life afterwards. When Agustin's headlights picked up her unmistakable red hair in the darkness, she had no way of knowing that both those weighty problems were soon to be resolved for her.

In the events that followed, no one bothered to consider the plight of the proprietor of the inn where

Agustin and Panchika passed the night. But a proprietor of an inn of doubtful reputation cannot expect mercy in this world.

Still, it was to his credit that he managed at least to save the life of Panchika. As soon as he smelled fumes from the faulty heater, he hurried upstairs to Agustin's room. When he opened the door, he must have realized it was the end for him as an innkeeper, as indeed it was.

The knowledge did not keep him from his duty, and it must be said he acted with a pathetic sort of decency as far as Panchika was concerned. When he found her alive beside the window to which she had crawled and even managed to open a crack, his first action was to slip her arms into her coat and button it over her nude body. Then he carried her downstairs to his car and to the house of the doctor in the village. There was no need to bother with Agustin. He was quite dead.

In time, Panchika was to make a recovery. Mercifully, she was spared the ordeal of convalescence under the inquiring eyes of the village. As soon as she was able, the doctor moved her to a hospital in distant Bordeaux. She remained there under the best care that money could buy. Then she was placed as a maid in a good home in Paris, and as far as I know, she is there today.

All this was taken care of in a quiet way by Agustin's father. He neither expected nor received any credit for it. For everyone's sake, it was simply something that had to be done. Panchika has never returned to the village even for a visit. And perhaps that is just as well, too.

If the decision had been left to the doyen, I know that the matter of Agustin's funeral would have been handled with discretion. But that wise man was not to return to the village until the next morning, when the damage had already been done.

The visit of Agustin's father to the vicar might have seemed to be bad timing. But in a country where there is no preserving of the dead, haste is necessary.

So it was that on the afternoon of the same day the young man's body was taken home, Agustin's father set out to make the arrangements. His first stop was to inquire into Panchika's condition and give the doctor instructions for her care. His next stop was at the carpenter's to order a coffin for his son. Then, he went to see the vicar about the funeral Mass.

It was once the practice in these mountain villages to bury the unrepentant at some crossroads. That was in a time when the churches owned the cemeteries. In a later day, the cemeteries became the property of the commune, and the churches lost the privilege of deciding who was worthy to be buried in hallowed ground.

But one other right remained to them in principle. It was a right that had not been invoked except in the memory of the oldest in the village. Agustin's father was neither that old nor that acquainted with such affairs.

He became acquainted in a hurry, however, when the vicar told him there would be no funeral Mass for his son. The old smuggler was stunned. Unable to divine that the vicar's white-faced denunciation of Agustin may have had other roots, he tried to argue. But in the face of what everyone knew, who could argue that Agustin had not died in a state of sin?

When argument failed, the old smuggler fell back on the only language he knew. He did not realize that the mention of a bribe would make it impossible for the doyen to reverse the decision of the vicar.

When the doyen came back from his trip that evening, he managed to gather quite a bit of information in the short distance between the outer ramparts of the village and the house where he and the vicar lived. Because the doyen had genuine affection for Panchika and felt that she had been making progress, the news of the tragedy at first pained him deeply. But a priest must think of the new dead first, and by the time he arrived at his house, his care was about Agustin's immortal soul.

There were also a few gaps in the story that he was curious about. He was not so much of a fool that he was unable to sense that the villagers had done some neat footwork in what they had told him. There was, for example, the business of how Panchika's parents had managed to find out so positively about her sins.

The doyen's sympathy for the vicar had been dwindling for a long time. In the beginning, he had tried to chide the vicar tactfully about sermons and the sacred confidence of the confessional. The vicar learned no lessons from these conversations, and the only lesson the doyen learned was an old one about the futility of talk with the righteous.

The last flicker of the doyen's compassion for the vicar went out that night. The old housekeeper had never heard a priest swear before, but the doyen made up for it ten times when he found out who it was that had informed on Panchika. Afterwards, in her telling of the encounter, the housekeeper could never make up her mind whether to be scandalized or impressed.

The swearing was unfortunate, however, in that it shored up the vicar's obstinacy. Having spent his wrath, the doyen could only fall back on simple incredulity when the vicar told him he had denied Agustin the right of a funeral Mass. When the doyen questioned the decision, the vicar retaliated by telling him about the offer of a bribe by Agustin's father. He also mentioned that he was prepared to make an issue of the whole affair with the bishop in Bayonne, whose reputation for strictness in these matters was legendary.

The doyen listened in silence. Never before in his priestly life had he been so challenged, but he was enough of a card player to know when the game was running against him. The doyen could see no way out.

He did not reckon, however, with outside intervention. This was to come in the shape of a thin little woman with the toughness of heart that goes with being a smuggler's wife.

In smuggling, as in most things, the secret of success lies in alternative. If the clever man cannot achieve his desired result in one way, he looks for another.

Agustin's father had not become a successful smuggler by accident. In his own field of contraband, which was liquors and Spanish lace, he was a master in the art of alternative. This stood for something in a frontier region where the occupation of smuggling was of vintage quality. A thousand deceptions had been practiced upon the government, and in time found out. It took a man of imagination and great memory to come up with the undiscovered deception or one that had been long forgotten.

Agustin's mother had not become the wife of a smuggler by chance, either. She had gone into the marriage with her eyes wide open, knowing its drawbacks and its rewards. But when one has been raised the daughter of a poor farm servant, the question of drawbacks is of small importance.

Finding herself so suddenly surrounded by wealth, she did not delude herself by confusing money with station. Smuggling might be an accepted occupation in the Basque country, but it is not a respected one. The old division of living within the law or outside of it still holds, and people must have their pecking order. Agustin's mother carried many hurts.

In defiance, she never flaunted her wealth. Her house was rich within the sanctuary of solid walls, and plain outside. She never missed daily morning Mass and rarely the evening vespers. And then there was the fact that her eldest son, Michel, had joined the priesthood. Only in this might some have found a sop to respectability.

Her one advantage over her husband was that she had a wider grasp of the alternative. He used it only in his dealings with his adversary, the established order of government. It had never occurred to him that the church was also an established order and could be an adversary, too.

Agustin's mother may have had a premonition that things would not go well between her husband and the vicar. She accepted the news with the same stoical silence with which she had heard other bad tidings in her life. When he wanted to talk about it, she merely said the conversation could wait until the family was all together. By that, she meant the arrival of the priest in the family.

She waited until Michel had cried away the edge of his grief beside the candle-lined coffin in the parlor where Agustin lay, more in repose than he had ever been in life. When that was done, she summoned Michel to the businesslike glare of the kitchen table and laid the facts coldly before him. She waited again until his outrage passed, and then asked him a few questions about those rules of the church with which she was not familiar.

Being a young priest, Michel's responses were obscured by theory. But finally, the answers came through. The mother heard them, nodded in confirmation of what she had expected, and then outlined their plan of action.

Michel was doubtful. He had not had much opportunity in his career to think for himself. She stilled his arguments with the reminder that it was not a stranger, but his brother, who was concerned here.

Agustin's father was not doubtful, but only amazed. As he said later when the wounds of loss had been healed, he could not help thinking what a remarkable success his wife would have made in his particular occupation.

The doyen had performed his morning offices with a dull heart. When he had awakened from a night of little sleep, it was to a vision of a young man's soul with nowhere to go. Agustin's body might be interred in hallowed ground, but without a funeral Mass, the vicar had made sure that Agustin's soul remained at the crossroads.

As if this were not enough weight to carry, the doyen sensed the difference in the villagers when he went for his morning stroll. How they had found out he did not take the trouble to divine. What mattered was that having found out, they did not like it. They were an ancient people with an ancient sense of right, and this to him was the hurtful thing. Not that it would affect their religion any, because that was also ancient in them, but it would affect their feeling toward him. One did not lose his parishioners. One only lost their respect.

Having avoided the vicar throughout the morning, the doyen had closed himself in his study. Wrestling with his emotions, it was only by instinct that he gathered something of importance was going on in the foyer. Vaguely, he had heard the knocker, and vaguely he had remembered that the housekeeper was on her shopping rounds. The sharp, nervous step of the vicar had sounded on its way to the door, and the doyen returned to the more serious problem of his own composure. But when the quality of the two voices in the foyer took on a subtle change, something propelled the doyen out of his chair and through the intervening door.

The visitor whose back was toward him was garbed in a priest's cassock, and for the moment, the doyen felt that his instinct had deceived him. Then the visitor turned.

When he closed the study door behind Michel, the doyen was aware that he had committed an affront in excluding the vicar. He was also aware that whatever lay so poorly concealed behind Michel's determined brow might add up to another affront to the vicar. The doyen suffered no qualms on either count. He was merely surprised that after preaching charity so long, his heart could be so sincerely uncharitable.

In making his request, Michel mentioned the weight of precedent often and his mother only once. But that once was enough to reveal to the doyen that precedent added up to nothing when it came to shoring up the backbone.

Michel did not need to present such a lengthy argument. The doyen would have given him permission in any case. The request to say a Mass for a departed soul was perfectly proper. That it would amount to a funeral Mass might have been open to challenge. But if the body was not present, then what was there to challenge? And if a blessing from a little church could find its long way to Heaven, it should not have much trouble finding the village square. After all, one could throw a rock that far.

In the morning of the next day, a funeral cortege bearing the body of Agustin made its slow way from the house of his parents. The coffin was draped with a pall of proper black, and it was followed by a proper procession of family and friends. Michel walked at the head of the coffin intoning the proper litany.

When the procession reached the village square, the coffin was set down on the cobblestones and remained there, flanked by two men with their heads uncovered. The rest filed into the church, and a Mass for the departed soul of Agustin was said by his brother. The doyen personally served as acolyte for Michel in the saying of the Mass. He could not, of course, accompany the procession from the church to the village square, and from there to the cemetery. But the gesture within the church was considered by the villagers to be enough.

The vicar did not participate in the Mass for Agustin's soul. For the few days he remained in the village, there were rumors he intended to take the matter of the subterfuge to the bishop in Bayonne. But there has been no reprimand of the doyen that I have heard of.

At the vicar's departure to another post, it was also rumored that the doyen gave him this bit of counsel—that religion with all its age and power is weaker than the tiny fact of a family.

Perhaps the vicar learned a new and lasting lesson. But when anyone ventures this hope, the villagers only shake their heads. They are not renowned as a romantic lot.

The Basque Beret

They say in the Basque country that the beret is dying.

They say it is the fault of the young, who do not regard the beret as fashionable anymore, who prefer to go bareheaded in all seasons, and who have no sense, anyway. They say the young don't realize what they are losing.

The men in the village say that when one considers all the uses of a beret, to lose it would be like losing a friend. In the summer, it protects the head from sunstroke and shields the eyes from glare. In the winter, its crown can be arranged so that it juts out over the forehead like a tent, so rain will drip to both sides of the nose instead of pouring directly upon it, which would be insupportable. In the farmyard, it can be used to gather eggs, and in the forest, chestnuts. At table, it guards the head from damps and draughts. And in bed, nothing could be more comfortable than placing one's cold feet upon a hot brick wrapped in a beret.

The women in the village bemoan its passing because it tells the temper of a man. If he is wearing it tipped back on his head, then he is happy and can be approached with demands. If he has pulled it down severely over his forehead, then his mood is bad and one must take caution. If it is tipped to one side, then a man is in a rakish humor and a wife will know it is no time to let him go into the village. But if he does, and comes home with his beret sitting like a pieplate on his head, then she will understand he is drunk.

Though I sympathize with the men in their loss, I know that in practical matters one can usually make do with other things. But when I consider the plight of the women, then I must conclude that their loss will be the graver.

A Spanish Mass

He was trudging back down the road from the Spanish frontier. The road is steep and winding, banked on one side by forests and thick growths of berry bushes, and dropping off on the other side to the river below. I saw him as I rounded the bend, and his gait was familiar.

"*Adio*," I said, drawing alongside. "Do you want a ride?"

"Well, I'm almost home now," he said with faint accusation, as if I should have happened by earlier. "It's hardly worth it."

Knowing that he had two more hours of walking, I urged him. He shrugged and got in.

He was a poor *paysan* from a tiny mountain farm beyond the village, and he bore the reputation of an irascible man. Nevertheless, he had taken pity and invited me into his house when a heavy rainstorm had caught me walking in the mountains. And I had stopped back for a glass of wine other times since.

"Have you been to Spain?" I asked him.

"That road doesn't go to Africa," he said.

He was a man with a thin, unshaven face and a beaked nose. He was wearing his Sunday best, a black coat and striped shirt that were probably handed down from his father, and a beret and rope sandals that were his own. "You're all dressed up," I said.

"Evidently," he said, and lapsed into a dour silence.

When we reached the village, I asked him to join me at the tavern for a glass of wine. He refused until I reminded him that I owed him many glasses of wine.

"Did you find Spain to be a nice country?" I said when his temper had mellowed.

"For Spaniards," he said.

"They are Basques up there," I said. "They're not Spaniards."

"They live in Spain, they are Spaniards," he said. "You sound like a Spanish priest."

When he realized that he had made a revealing slip, he had a moment of chagrin. Then he shrugged in defeat and told me the story.

The *paysan* had saved for a long time to set aside a little hoard of money for a special purpose. When he calculated that he had enough, he walked the long miles to a point near the Spanish frontier. There, he had waited until night to cross the river by the old wooden bridge. Otherwise, he would have had to produce a passport in order to cross the new bridge at the frontier. He slept that night in the forest, and at daybreak, found his way to the frontier village and the house where the priest lived. "That priest was not in a good temper, simply because I woke him up," the *paysan* said. "They are lazy in Spain, you know."

I nodded and he went on:

"I told the priest that I wanted a Spanish Mass offered, and I was careful to assure him that I had the money to pay for it.

"The priest said to me, 'There is no such thing as a Spanish Mass. And anyway, I am Basque.'

"I said to him, 'You live in Spain, you are a Spaniard.'

"The priest was irritated, but he didn't risk arguing the point. Instead, he said, 'But why have you come all the way here to request a Mass? Your own village priest would accommodate you.'

"So I told him, 'I will not even ask my own priest, because he will certainly refuse.'

"And the priest raised his eyes to Heaven and said, 'Things are worse in France than I imagined.'

"Allowing that insult to pass, I took out my money and we fixed the date when the Spanish Mass was to be said. The priest took the money easily enough, you can be sure of that. But then, when I was ready to leave, he said to me, 'I know that the Mass is to be for a private intention. But for my own guidance, can you inform me if it is for a loved one who is dead?'

"So I said to the priest, 'He is not a loved one. He is my neighbor, and he is not dead. Not yet, anyway.'

"And the priest said to me, 'Oh, then your neighbor is ailing.'

"I said to the priest, 'No, he is in good health. At least he thinks so.'

"The priest would not let go of it, and he said, 'You mean your neighbor believes he is in good health, but you know differently. That is indeed solicitous of you.'

"And I said to the priest, 'No, I don't know differently. But I expect to in a few days.'

"The priest said, 'I don't understand. How do you expect to know in a few days?'

"So I said to the priest, 'Well, I have to see if the Mass takes.'

"And the priest said, 'I don't understand you at all.''

"So I told the priest, 'My neighbor is my enemy. I want him dead, and that's why I have ordered a Mass.'

"The priest was shocked, if you can imagine it. And he said, 'I can't offer a Mass against your enemy. How dare you suggest that I could do anything like that?'

"So I said to the priest in all honesty, 'Because it is well known that a Spanish priest will do anything for money.' "

We sipped our wine in silence. Suspecting the end of the *paysan's* story, I asked him, "Did he throw you out?"

"That's a hard way to put it," the *paysan* said petulantly. "But he's not fooling me one bit. When I go back next time, I'll have enough money. I know my Spanish priests."

La Guerre
est Terminée

The limping postman recognized the German this morning where he sat sketching on the terrace of the hotel.

The German commandant had come back to the village in a pathetic sort of disguise—a flowered shirt and dark glasses. He was young no longer, but faltering and stoop-shouldered, with a thin, proud mouth and the luminous gray hair of one who had once been very blond.

He returned last night when the village was asleep, and this afternoon, he left as quietly as he had come. There has been little else talked about in the shops and taverns. It is as though all the intervening years had not existed, and the war had ended only yesterday.

The villagers talk about how it was when the first convoy came. Except for the rumbling of the trucks, there had been absolutely no sound and no motion. The Germans passed through a silent street, and silent dark-garbed people lined up in front of silent buildings.

The mayor had waited for the Germans in the village square. There had been the clatter of heavy boots on cobblestones and the clank of machine guns and rifles. The mayor had neither proferred his hand nor taken off his beret. The German commandant asked the mayor if the people's attitude should be interpreted as a promise of resistance. The mayor gestured to the fortress looming over the village, a fortress that had at various times been occupied by a Roman commander, a Spanish commander, and a French commander. *You are not the first invader to have passed through here,* the mayor said. *We will not fight you. We will endure you.*

The Germans found out what he meant. On the farms, provisions given on demand but never volunteered. In the bars, liquor served without words. Curfew observed in the streets, but never in the houses. With the men, work performed but never without demand for payment. With the women, approaches made but never acknowledged. Conversations that began in French, but when a soldier was near, retreated to the impenetrable Basque language.

The commandant had started it badly enough, at that. Because the orders were to live off the country and his men had no mattresses on which to sleep, he commandeered them from the houses.

On one little farm on the outskirts of the village, a *paysan* with a World War I moustache said to him, *I served in the occupation in Alsace-Lorraine and we never stooped to this.* And the German commandant answered, *That was peace, and this is war.* And the *paysan* said, *Here, it is not war. You know nothing of war. It has been so easy for you.*

After that, the *paysan* waged his own kind of passive war by spoiling everything he was required to turn over to them. Soured wine and rotting vegetables and badly cured pork guaranteed to wreak havoc with the digestion. And in the idle times, he sent his half-witted son to steal the soldiers' clothes when they were playing rugby or swimming in the river, so that each game and each swim were interrupted several times by pursuit of a boy who could neither be reasoned with nor, in conscience, punished.

The commandant could have ignored the *paysan*'s private little war, except that it did not remain private very long. When the example began to be picked up by the others, he had no recourse but to punish the *paysan*. But since he could prove nothing of intent, he resorted to the ridiculous punishment of marching his troops back and forth over the *paysan*'s vegetable garden until everything was mashed into pulp. That bit of child's play had not raised the commandant's standing any among the villagers.

Nor had his love of painting, which he resurrected to ease the boredom of occupation. It had been a ludicrous sight to see a man in polished boots and stiff military uniform performing a poetic task. And so the commandant had to retreat into the countryside to find seclusion to paint.

I suspect the painting worked the change in him. He had painted on wintry Pyrenean days when gray skies pressed down on bare forests of oak and chestnut, and blue smoke wreathed upwards from a hundred chimneys to fuse with the gray. He had painted on summer days when the valley with its strange diffusion of light was so blinding with color that he had remarked he had never known the true quality of green before.

It was in this time of unlocked vision that the commandant became interested in the people. It was a natural progression. One could not paint an environment without finally wondering about its inhabitants.

This was when he took it upon himself to relax his own rule. The people were to be treated fairly in all things. Little by little, the villagers had responded in kind until the day came when the mayor said to him, *I don't know your reasons, but I will say you are treating us with fairness.*

Then suddenly the war had gone badly for the Germans. Workers were needed at home in Germany, and for the first time there was the cold aspect of trucks lined up in the street to rob a village of its young men.

It did not stop there. Soldiers had been turned to scrapmongering, to stripping monuments dedicated to the dead of one war so that the bronze could be melted down to provide the dead of another war. After that, the Germans confiscated the bicycles. And one night they shot a boy whose bicycle was dear enough to him to risk fleeing from a patrol. The boy's life was saved, but it was small comfort for a family whose father had been killed on the Maginot line and whose other sons had died in work camps in Germany.

There was a little building in the village that had been used as a provisional jail. Its constant occupant was a soldier named Willie, who was good natured but a drunk. There was a smooth cement wall with a tiny barred window on the side of the building, and the boys of the village played handball against it. Willie had whiled away his days throwing back the handballs that came through the barred window.

It was from Willie that the villagers first learned that the Germans were leaving. He said to the children, *I am going away with the rest. To the Russian front. Goodbye. All is lost now. We are beaten.*

He had been right. And so had the *paysan* with the World War I moustache, who stationed himself by the side of the road to watch the soldiers leave the village. When the German commandant passed, the *paysan* had called out to him, *Now you will find out something of war.*

The postman recognized the German commandant this morning as he sat sketching on the hotel terrace across the street from the ramparts. The postman had reason to remember. It was he who had lost a father in battle and two brothers in German labor camps. And it was he who had been shot because his bicycle was dear to him.

The postman crossed the street to the hotel terrace, driving his crippled leg in front of him with the tenacity of one who must live by immediate destinations. He was carrying a worn leather pouch attached to a strap looped across his chest, and his left hand rested in the recesses of the pouch.

The postman approached the German commandant and said, "There is a letter for you."

The German watched the hand come out of the worn leather pouch and lay the unstamped envelope on the table in front of him.

The postman said, "It is a letter from a family. Unfortunately, it was not possible for the father and the oldest sons to sign it, since they are dead. I have taken the liberty of doing it in their absence."

The German did not bother even to open the letter. He must have known instantly that it was a threat of death. He said simply, "I understand." Then he went into the hotel, and a few minutes later, walked with his suitcase to where his car was parked in the shadow of the ramparts.

The villagers cannot understand how the German commandant could have dared to come back in the first place. I can tell them why. He had made the mistake of thinking the war was long enough over. And his heart had forgotten to accompany him when he left here.

Peace

We had come down to the meadow together, clambering over the wooden pole gate and walking through the waving grass. And together we had explored the old stone ruin of a little house beside the stream.

The house had been caught up by time, or worse, and its crumbled walls were very nearly enveloped by vines and shrouding brier. We found a room in which a family once had lived, but the roof above the room was open now to the sky. Rubble had covered a table with only two legs left standing, and it had filled a battered cradle beside the hearth. Afterwards, we had each gone our wordless way back to the sun in the meadow.

The grass in this meadow is marvelously deep, so that where I am lying it is as soft as the softest bed, and the crushed green smell of it rises around me. The meadow slopes down to the stream, and from where I am lying I can see my wife and my children below me. I cannot see them distinctly, but as in a dream, because it is through a veil of waving grass.

Bruce is lying beside the stream, and I can see only his blond head resting on his crossed hands. He is watching the water flow over the shining pebbles.

The meadow is filled with a multitude of tiny flowers, and Monique and her mother are making chains of golden buttercups and white marguerites.

When the wind blows in the meadow, the deep grass bends to show the softness of its underside in long undulating ripples. Kristin is chasing the ripples in the grass. Her flaxen braids fly in the wind and her perfect little face is flushed, and she is laughing. The tinkle of her laughter is the only sound in the world.

Jean Pierre's America

Jean Pierre is first neighbor to my cousin. Their farms lie side by side, so in the old tradition they are obliged to help each other in times of haying and planting. It is in these times that I see him.

Jean Pierre loves America with a passionate zeal. In fact, I have never in my life known anyone who loves America as much as Jean Pierre.

Ten years ago, Jean Pierre went to America to work as a milker on a farm near Los Angeles. He lived in a bunkhouse there and milked two hundred cows a day, working sixteen hours out of the twenty-four, and six days out of the seven. With the money he saved, he returned to the Basque country, bought a farm and married, and already has two children. To accomplish all this in ten years is a feat in itself, and he must be admired for it.

Because Jean Pierre loves America, he is a source of much embarrassment to me. Whenever we have respites in the haying, all that Jean Pierre wants to talk about is America. During these times, of course, my cousin is audience.

"Oh, how I loved it there!" Jean Pierre says. "I didn't cry when I left here, but I assure you that I cried when I left there."

When Jean Pierre says this, I can see my cousin

bridling, so I say, "But this is a beautiful country, too."

Jean Pierre dismisses my argument with a wave of his hand. "This poor country? It is nothing when one considers the richness of America."

And then Jean Pierre talks at length about the great farms of America, the thousands of cows, the high office buildings and millions of cars and the magnificent highways of Los Angeles. He speaks of these things with an air of possession, as if he had owned them all himself.

My cousin, who has traveled, says irritably, "Well, we have great farms in France, too, and there are big office buildings and millions of cars in Paris."

But Jean Pierre, who has never seen Paris, dismisses his argument, too, with a wave of his hand and the words, "It is nothing when one considers the richness of America."

When they argue like this, I remain very silent because there is really nothing I can say, and I am relieved when Jean Pierre begins to digress.

"I would have gone back to America," Jean Pierre says sadly. "But I happened to get married, and so I stayed here. I didn't know my wife before I left, and I don't know her now, either. It takes seven years to know a woman, they say, and sometimes seventy-seven."

I know that a man must have the right to believe that he had an alternative. That is simply a protection.

But I have seen Jean Pierre's wife. She is a dark-haired beauty with laughing eyes that see only him, and I know Jean Pierre could not have done better. And I have seen his farm, too. He has a home of whitewashed stone that is finer than twenty bunk-houses, a shining new tractor, and waving fields of hay and grain that he does not have to speak of in implied tones of possession, because they really belong to him.

But when one considers the richness of Jean Pierre's America, all this is nothing.

Haying Time

Always it seems that when we hay, we are rushing to beat the rain.

This morning when we began, the sky was blue and the day was clear and so we were deceived. We should have known when we were turning the fallen hay, because the flies flew up in swarms from their dark, green, hiding places and took their vengeance on us. My cousin's *domestique* also knew, because he is terrified of storms and was shaking his head ominously even when the sky was blue. But he is simpleminded, and so we paid no attention to him.

By midday, there was a thickness in the air that made it difficult to breathe, and our bodies were drenched with unnatural sweat. When the first clouds nosed over the mountain we began to work more furiously. We hoisted our pitchforks heavy with hay to the top of the wagon until our arms were ready to crack, and then goaded the oxen to the barn in a rumbling trot. And inside the vast interior of the barn, we created sweet-smelling mountains of hay with little paths running between.

By the time there was only one wagon-load left, the sky was dark with clouds, and the air was charged with blue light. And then suddenly the lightning ripped the sky apart and the thunder went off with the sound of artillery fire. With the first roar, my cousin's *domestique* was gone with his hands clapped over his ears, and no amount of shouting could bring him back.

When the first big drops of rain began to fall, the wagon was nearly full. We stayed until the last moment, and then men and oxen and wagon made a dash across the field and up the ramp to the barn. By the time we reached it, the rain had soaked us to the skin. But it washed away the hay dust and the sweat and the tiredness that had been tearing at our limbs.

And afterwards, we sat near the open doorway to the house and drank warming wine and ate huge quantities of bread and sausage and watched the pouring rain and laughed because we had run a race with a storm, and won.

Ramon

Ramon is my cousin's *domestique*.

In body, Ramon is a man. His chest is deep and his arms are strong and he has a constant beard that never seems to grow beyond a stubble.

When Ramon was a child, he had meningitis, and it left him with the mind of a child. It left its mark in other ways, too.

One of them is that Ramon is never sick. He works in the cold and damps with nothing to protect him except a thin shirt. But Ramon is afraid of storms and falling elements. If he is working in the fields and it begins to rain, he runs for cover with his hands clasped on top of his beret. When it thunders, he puts his hands over his ears and runs to his stone hovel and closes the door against the sound. He is not afraid of snow, but this is because he has a special costume for protection. It is a red stocking cap that my aunt knitted for him. The cap fits over his head and covers his face so that only his eyes show. And on top of this, he plants his beret like a pie plate.

Ramon's stone hovel is a shed attached to the rear wall of the farmhouse. In this dark cave, there is only a straw pallet, a tiny stove, and a nail on the wall for his one pair of trousers and one shirt. His wooden shoes rest neatly together beneath. On the stove, he brews his morning coffee and toasts his bread. But in the evenings, he simply eats what my aunt has brought him in a warm plate. He does not know how to read, he speaks only a child's Basque, and French is a foreign language to him. So, when his evening meal is done, he goes directly to bed to await the next day's work.

Work is Ramon's only satisfaction in life. He tends the garden more carefully than any woman, and he is tireless in the fields, so much so that he is always disappointed when the day's work is done.

My cousin treats him decently. He understands that work is Ramon's only satisfaction and his only reason for pride. He compliments Ramon for work well done, and Ramon responds like a dutiful child who wants to do things right.

When the family leaves the farm even to go to the village, Ramon is sad. He mopes in the distance and cries big tears until they have returned. Sometimes at night, when he hears their voices in the kitchen of the main house, he pounds on the wall with his fist until someone calls out to him. Then Ramon is comforted and can sleep.

Today, when we were haying in the fields, my cousin thought it would be a great adventure for Ramon to guide the loaded wagon back to the barn. He said to Ramon, "You have watched me enough times. It will be easy for you."

Ramon shook his head, refusing. But the expression in his eyes said that he was tempted. So my cousin went through the motions of showing Ramon how to start the oxen with the goad, how to lay the wooden staff on the side of the oxen's heads to make them turn, and finally how to lay the staff across their heads in front of the yoke to make them stop. After that, he handed the staff to Ramon, and Ramon did not refuse it.

From the end of the field, there is a rutted path that rises sharply to the haybarn. This part of the passage must be maneuvered carefully, because there is an overhanging limb that barely manages to clear the top of a load of hay. Ramon guided the oxen across the field well enough, but the first doubt came into his eyes when the wagon started up the rutted path.

"Careful, now," my cousin warned as the wagon neared the limb. Perhaps he should not have called the warning, and perhaps it would have happened anyway.

Ramon failed to turn the oxen at the precise moment, and the limb sliced through the load of hay. It was like the beginning of an avalanche in which one is powerless to do anything but stand and watch. The hay cascaded down the sloping side and over Ramon, until half the load was gone. I caught one glimpse of his stricken face before he was buried in hay. He came up out of it like a swimmer sputtering in water. When he saw the havoc that he had made, he sat down on the ground and dug his man's knuckles into his child's eyes and cried out in anguish, "What pain! What pain!"

My cousin is usually contained. Now, for a moment, I thought that he had lost his senses. He bolted up the path to the toolshed and emerged with an axe. Leaping up the trunk of the tree, he fastened himself in a crotch and began taking mighty blows at the offending limb. Ramon raised his tear-stained eyes and stopped crying to watch. Chips flew everywhere. The limb sagged and fell. My cousin leaped down and threw it to one side with distaste.

Ignoring Ramon, he said to me with a stern voice, "I have told myself a hundred times that I must cut that limb. Do you see now what procrastination can lead to?"

Picking up a pitchfork, he began heaving the fallen hay onto the wagon as methodically and unhurriedly as if he were in the field. I joined him. And in a little while, so did Ramon.

Heavy Crosses

The procession had formed at the crossroads that mark the junction of five villages. There, in the cool of the summer morning, they had begun the long pilgrimage to the monastery on top of the mountain.

At the head of the procession were the acolytes with their silver crosses and the silk banner of the Virgin, its tapestry faded with age. Then came the vicar in his robes, walking under a canopy worked with gold and silver thread. And after him came the mayors of the five villages, resplendent in their crimson-lined cloaks, frilled white collars, and knee-length breeches of times before.

But the most impressive in the procession were those who came next. They were the sturdy young men of the villages, covered from view with ominous black robes and peaked black hoods broken only by eyeslits. On their backs, they carried heavy wooden crosses.

When they passed this morning, their fervor was inspiring. The vicar led the singing in a strong voice, and the acolytes chanted the responses with great reverence. The mayors walked proud as peacocks, and behind them the hooded men carried their crosses as if they were made of straw.

The procession emptied into the cavernous depths of the monastery chapel. And when Mass was done, the participants emptied out again. The priest and his acolytes went to lunch in the monastery, and the mayors and young men descended upon the only restaurant. There, they indulged in food and wine, shouted and sang, and flirted with the girls who had come to watch the procession.

Now, it is late afternoon and the procession is making its way home. The vicar walks under the canopy with his hands clasped in front of him, but once in a while he stumbles. The acolytes sing the responses, but now the chanting is more like a dirge.

And as for the young men in hoods and cloaks, their crosses have become noticeably heavier.

Old Man Alone

He was an old man and he was very drunk.

He had come out of a tavern which is tucked against the stone ramparts in such a way that the wall of the rampart is also the back wall of the tavern. They must have asked him to leave, because after he had come out, the lights in the tavern were turned off for the night.

Because he was drunk, and crippled, too, the old man made his way toward the street with difficulty. He must have been badly crippled, because he was hoisting himself along with two short crutches of the kind that clamp around the wrists. Still, his arms were strong. One cannot lift the weight of a body as big as his without having good arms.

The street that he was trying to cross was wide. It was the main street of the village, and it was illuminated by a single streetlamp on a high arching pole. He had made his way to the center of the circle of light when he stopped and looked about him in surprise, because suddenly there were people in the street. The vesper hour had ended in the village church, and the girls and women were emptying into the street on their way home.

When he saw himself surrounded, he made as gracious a bow as his condition permitted. And then he began to sing a song. He sang only to the girls, because they stopped while their mothers passed him by with silent disapproval.

The song he sang was a courting song, and it was daring in the manner of the old Basque. He sang it very well and richly, and he accompanied his serenade with gestures, bracing himself on one crutch and waving the other in the air like an overlong arm.

The girls listened to his song with giggling, and when he was through they clapped their hands in applause. But they did not mock him, except perhaps that they clapped too loudly. Encouraged by that, he began another song. But the girls heeded the beckoning of their mothers and went their scattered ways home. In an instant, the street was deserted again and there was no one to listen to the old man.

Slowly, he made his way across the street to the other side. In the shadow line between light and darkness, he stopped again to sing. But this time he did not stand erect. His head was bent and his song was the lament of an old man alone.

Youths' Song

In the evening, I had made my way along the green river to the Roman bridge that marks the end of the village. The air was soft and summer sweet, and I sat on the simple stone arch and dangled my legs over the water and watched quiet dusk descend upon the village.

The shepherd boy had come down from the mountain by some hidden path. The first I knew of his coming was when suddenly the evening was filled with his whistling. It was a lovely trilling torrent of song. It was a bursting song of youth and joy on a summer evening.

The shepherd boy came into view, a slender shadow with a shaggy little dog at his heels. He came down the path with his head thrown back and with a sandaled step so light that he did not seem even to be touching the ground. Believing himself to be all alone, he stopped on the path and, twirling his shepherd's staff around him and whistling with the sound of a hundred flutes, did a solitary dance in the dusk.

And then he saw me, and it was as if an arrow had pierced the breast of a bird. How sad it is to have stilled the song of a boy. And sadder yet to have heard the song of youth on a summer's evening and to remember how it once had been.

Ancestors

I have walked through a hundred graveyards in this tiny land and read the lineage of a hundred villages.

The crosses bear the names of my people. They surround the churches like flowers shaped in stone. If they are cared for, they stand upright. If they are not cared for, they begin to lean. If they fall, they are moved to the edge of the churchyard to rest against the stone wall and join those whose family successions have ended.

There are other tombstones abandoned against the wall. They are round with primitive carvings from that time when my people lingered between a Christian God and the old religion of sun and moon and seasons.

A thousand generations of my ancestors have gone down into this ground. Sometimes when I walk through the aisles of stone, the smell of the ground rises up. It is old and familiar, and I know instantly that this ground is in me.

I have been buried here in a hundred little graveyards.